MW01291539

Concepts of the United States Constitution

Douglas V. Gibbs

CONSTITUTION ASSOCIATION PRESS • MURRIETA, CALIFORNIA

To those who seek the truth…
The truth always leads those who seek it to the same conclusions.

CONTENTS

INTRODUCTION

There are certain constitutional concepts that are unnamed in the United States Constitution, but exist as a part of the American System. Some of these concepts are within the authorities granted by the United States Constitution, and some of them are not. This book identifies, categorizes, and describes these concepts. This book serves as a companion to two other books by Douglas V. Gibbs, *25 Myths of the United States Constitution*, and *The Basic Constitution: An Examination of the Principles and Philosophies of the United States Constitution*.

Concepts of the United States Constitution is divided into three parts. Part One covers constitutional unnamed concepts, and Part Two examines unconstitutional concepts that have been considered constitutional as a result of court rulings and opinions. Part Three examines concepts that may be constitutional in one sense, but are commonly used or portrayed in a manner that is not constitutional.

As more Americans begin to understand the truth about how our Constitution has been usurped by a ruling elite determined to fundamentally change America to a system the Founding Fathers never intended, the reality that we maintain a number of preconceived assumptions about what is and is not constitutional, is becoming more apparent. We have been blind our entire lives, subject to a life-long indoctrination.

The world of the Founding Fathers was very similar to ours in the sense that they were facing an unreasonable tyranny that considered the rights of the people to be a minor obstacle to the goals of the ruling elite. The colonists, however, considered themselves to be English Freemen, a concept supported by their Saxon heritage, the Magna Carta, and the English Bill of Rights of 1689.

Like the Founders, we have historical reference that confirms our heritage of liberty, if only we would be willing to recognize it, and perform the eternal vigilance required to protect it. Unfortunately, human nature has proven to be an obstacle. Throughout history, tyranny is the norm, and liberty is the exception. The enemies of constitutionally mandated limited government have controlled education, information, entertainment, and the news media, and when a people have endured such a life-long indoctrination, it is difficult for an individual to examine new ideas, and be willing to participate in enacting dramatic corrective change to the system we live in.

Understanding human nature, the opposition to the principles of the Constitution have altered the American System systematically and incrementally. We have been trained to view the news of the world the way they have instructed us to view it. We have been convinced that our freedom has contributed to the misery and strife in the world, and to save the world, we must become as miserable as our fellow global citizens.

Statism is a system of beliefs that opposes the concepts of individualism and liberty, a religion designed to alter society, and abolish all opposition to its utopian dreams of collectivism and communal economics. It alters language, redefines terms, and promises that the aim of statism is truth and justice, when in reality only bondage can come of it. The statists call for social justice, economic justice, environmental justice, and racial justice, when justice has little to do with the finality they seek.

Totalitarian regimes have emerged and collapsed throughout history. Each of them consider themselves to be new, or different, but in the end their allegiance to statism has always been the same. The dictators viewed themselves as being members of a political elite who alone knew what was best for society. In those oligarchies, individualism was viewed as being dangerous, perhaps even treasonous. Individuals think for themselves, rebel against authority when the conditions seem less than favorable for them. Rebellious individuals can be dangerous to the oligarchy, so oligarchies are always quick to remove from the members of the population the ability to defend themselves. That is what tyrannical governments do. They disarm the people, and then remove the educated from society, because behind the curtain, the reality is that the powerful few are fearful. They are fearful of losing their position, and power.

Those who understand history, and are informed about political systems, are dangerous to the continued reign of a tyrannical regime. It is the duty of the educated and the informed to protect the Blessings of Liberty, and teach the next generation to do the same. James Madison told us that "A well-instructed people alone can be permanently a free people."

The aim of this book is to play a part in the education of the public so that the individuals of American Society may properly arm themselves with the tools constitutionally available to restore, if possible, the republic.

The original forging of the United States marked a change from the tyrannical ideas of the Old World. America was a radically liberal (in the terms of classical liberalism) concept, an experiment the elitists of Europe were sure would fail. In the minds of the ruling elite in Europe, self-governance was impossible. The people were not capable of successfully navigating the waters of governance.

The United States of America proved the Old World statists wrong. . . for a while.

Part One

Constitutional Concepts

CHAPTER 1

LIMITED GOVERNMENT

The United States Constitution was written with the recognition that too small of a government, as we had under the Articles of Confederation, would not properly protect, preserve and promote the union of States that had just won their independence from the British Empire. Too large of a government would surely lead to tyranny. Under the Articles of Confederation, the United States Government was as weak as a lamb. What the new country needed was a lion. The problem with lions, though, is that lions eat you. So, the task before the Founding Fathers during the Constitutional Convention in 1787 was to create a lion, but cage it and restrain it in such a way that the people, and the Blessings of Liberty, are protected from that lion.

In Europe, most of the governments were authoritarian. The monarchies were oligarchies, with a absolute monarch serving as the figure head, and consuls serving as advisors with the intention of maintaining a powerful rule over the people. The former English colonies had just fought a war against a tyrannical system. The leaders of the new United States researched the failures of the statist systems in Europe, and the statist oligarchies throughout history. The Founding Fathers had no intention of creating another failed, authoritarian government.

In 2010, after a debate regarding local politics, I was asked about my definition of "limited government." The challenge was presented by a potential constituent when I ran a campaign for a seat on my local city council. During the debate I repeatedly argued that my platform's foundation was based on the principles of limited government. A gentleman approached me afterward and asked, "You say you are in favor of our city having a limited government. So, what are you going to take away? The senior center? Parks?"

At first, I was confused. Why would I wish to remove these vital services from the people of my city?

After a lengthy conversation, I finally realized that the problem wasn't "limited government," but the gentleman's personal definition of what limited government is. According to him, limited government is smaller government, with things taken away until finally there is no government at all. My definition, however, differed greatly from his.

I explained to the gentleman that limited government, from the point of view of the United States Constitution, is government that operates within the authorities granted to it. The Founding Fathers never intended for the federal government to be a runaway entity that acts as it chooses, despite the rule of law. The federal government was designed to operate within the expressly enumerated authorities granted to it, and not beyond them.

When government expands beyond the limitations afforded to it, adding powers that were never granted, the government is "seizing" power without gaining the authority to possess it. A government that seizes power is not only one that is acting in a lawless manner, beyond the rule of law, and acting as if it is above the law, but by definition a government that seizes power is a tyranny.

Thomas Jefferson recognized the dangers of a strong central government, and suspected that even with the Constitution in place, we may see a bloody revolution in the United States every twenty years. That observation was the first part of his now often repeated quote, "The tree of liberty must be refreshed from time to time with the blood of patriots and tyrants."

James Madison saw government as being an evil that is a necessary part of society. He wrote in Federalist Paper No. 51, "If men were angels, no government would be necessary. If angels were to govern men, neither external nor internal controls on government would be necessary. In framing a government which is to be administered by men over men, the great difficulty lies in this: you must first enable the government to control the governed; and in the next place oblige it to control itself. A dependence on the people is, no doubt, the primary control on the government; but experience has taught mankind the necessity of auxiliary precautions."

The auxiliary precautions that Madison refers to are the limitations, coupled with various checks and balances, used in the writing of the Federal Constitution.

The true miracle of the Constitution is that the delegates who conducted the Constitutional Convention in 1787 were largely made up of men who desired "big government."

John Taylor, in his book, *A New View of the Constitution of the United States*, published in 1823, explains that the intent of the delegates was originally to create a "national government," but "The proposed national form of government was ultimately renounced or rejected." Despite the large contingent of nationalists in the convention, and the battle between whether the government should be a national one, or a federal one, the arguments presented by those that would later become known as "anti-federalists," and the reality of the potential of tyranny should the government be a national one, by the end of June in 1787, the delegates had largely surrendered to the understanding that the new government had to be a federal government limited to a small list of authorities, checks and balances inserted within the system, and the sovereignty of the several States.

The limited powers granted to the federal government were vested in the government by the States. As Mr. Taylor wrote, "In the creation of the federal government, the States exercised the highest act of sovereignty, and they may, if they please, repeat the proof of their sovereignty by its annihilation."

From the very beginning, those supporting a national government, a strong central government not limited by a constitution, have worked to deconstruct the original language, to compromise the sovereignty of the States, and to convince the public at large that the Constitution is nothing more than a guideline, a living and breathing document that can be changed at the whim of society, and the opinions of politicians and judges.

A government that does not operate within the limitations granted by a set standard such as a constitution is one that is not limited, but can do as it pleases without any restraints or restrictions.

The lion can be a powerful one if allowed to roam without any limitations. Its shackles and cage are the words of the U.S. Constitution. Without the principles of limited government provided by the Constitution, the federal government will be a tyranny with no limits, with no checks against its abuses of power.

In Federalist No. 39, James Madison wrote, "Each

State, in ratifying the Constitution, is considered as a sovereign body, independent of all others, and only to be bound by its own voluntary act. In this relation, then, the new Constitution will, if established, be a FEDERAL, and not a NATIONAL constitution."

In response to the concept that Congress can constitutionally pass any law they consider to be for the general welfare of the country, James Madison wrote to Edmund Pendleton, January 21, 1792, "If Congress can do whatever in their discretion can be done by money, and will promote the General Welfare, the Government is no longer a limited one, possessing enumerated powers, but an indefinite one, subject to particular exceptions."

In Federalist Paper No. 45, James Madison wrote, "The powers delegated by the proposed Constitution to the federal government are few and defined. Those which are to remain in the State governments are numerous and indefinite."

The federal government was created with the intent to be one that is limited, meaning that it was designed to be a government that operates within the authorities granted by the United States Constitution. Historically, when a government is limited, operating within its authorities, the society is prosperous, and the people enjoy the Blessings of Liberty.

CHAPTER 2

SEPARATION OF POWERS

Article I, Section 1 of the United States Constitution reads, "All legislative Powers herein granted shall be vested in a Congress of the United States, which shall consist of a Senate and House of Representatives."

Article II, Section 1 of the United States Constitution reads, "The executive Power shall be vested in a President of the United States of America."

Article III, Section 1 of the United States Constitution reads, "The judicial Power of the United States, shall be vested in one supreme Court, and in such inferior Courts as the Congress may from time to time ordain and establish."

The provision of "Separation of Powers" is not explicitly expressed by the United States Constitution, but the concept is presented and defined by the language used in the first sentence of each of the first three articles of the document.

James Madison, while he and George Mason were constructing the original draft of the Bill of Rights, included a proposed amendment that would make the separation of powers explicit, but the proposal was rejected. His colleagues in Congress expressed that the principle of the separation of powers was implicit in the structure of government under the language presented by the United States Constitution. Madison's proposed amendment, they concluded, would be a redundancy, and was unnecessary.

Separation of Powers was an important part of the principles presented by Montesquieu's concept of a mixed constitution. Montesquieu was a French political philosopher during the middle 1700s. Thomas Jefferson, as well as many of the other influential voices during the founding of this nation, were acquainted with Montesquieu's work, and were favorable of his ideas.

The idea of a mixed constitution was originally a concept introduced by a Greek historian named Polybius, who was deported to Rome after Greece fell to the Roman Empire. He admired the representative government of the Roman Republic. The era of Rome as a republic, however, was coming to an end, and statists who lusted for power were engaged in policies that would ultimately destroy the system of freedom, and turn Rome into a tyrannical empire. Polybius worked to restore honest government through the principles of the Roman Tablets. Polybius recommended a mixed constitution that blended the best of the three types of government in existence: a monarchy, aristocracy, and democracy. By themselves these types of government were unable to provide for equality, prosperity, justice, or domestic tranquility for the whole society. A mixed system, using the best traits of the three types of government, Polybius reasoned, would ensure freedom, and provide protection for individual rights. Though his philosophy began to develop in the Roman system, the dream of a three-department government ended with his death. After the demise of Polybius, the Romans began to abandon their principles of a republic.

During the middle 1700s, France's Baron Charles de Montesquieu worked to resurrect the concept of a mixed constitution, and resubmit it for the consideration of modern man with one addition.

Montesquieu added the idea of a separation of powers.

"There can be no liberty where the legislative and executive powers are united in the same person."

Montesquieu's writings were never popular in his homeland of France because his essays and book were so full of praise for the English system of government. In England, the Saxon system of government based its foundation on an individual-centric society, where no person, including the king, was above the law. The English system promoted freedom, personal rights, and a free market, rather than an authoritarian monarchy guided by an authoritarian religious system.

Though Montesquieu's book detailing his thoughts regarding a mixed constitution, and the separation of powers, never became popular in France, his book was greatly admired by the men in the English Colonies who had declared independence, and were forging a new nation. The political concepts offered by Montesquieu illuminated the minds of the Founders, encouraging them to create a system based on "separated" powers, guided by the consent of the governed, and containing a series of checks and balances.

Polybius recognized the three departments of government as being the executive, the senate, and the people's assembly. Montesquieu, however, saw his version of the separation of powers developing in England. Montesquieu's system of government developed along the lines of an executive, a legislature (with an upper and lower house), and an independent judiciary.

Montesquieu wrote, "When the legislative and executive powers are united in the same person, or in the same body of magistrates, there can be no liberty; because apprehensions may arise, lest the same monarch OR senate [legislature] should enact tyrannical laws, to execute them in a tyrannical manner. . . Again, there is no liberty, if the judiciary power be not separated from the legislative and executive. Were it joined with the legislative, the life and liberty of the subjects would be exposed to arbitrary control, for the judge would then be the legislator. Were it joined to the executive power, the judge might behave with violence and oppression."

Montesquieu called for a single executive, as opposed to the two or more consuls in Rome set up to preside over the people, or the thirty executives in Greece. A single executive would ensure responsibility would be concentrated in a single person who can make decisions quickly and decisively, and cannot escape either credit nor blame for the consequences.

The Framers of the Constitution feared giving any part of government too much power, and even placed in the Constitution certain checks and balances to reinforce the idea of "separation of powers." The prohibition of the use of "bills of attainder" in Article I, Section 9, for example, forbids the legislature from performing a judicial function.

The primary supporting evidence regarding the concept of Separation of Powers is found in the first sentence of each of the first three articles of the Constitution, as provided at the beginning of this chapter. The words were chosen carefully, with the original intent of ensuring that the powers given to each of the three branches of government were retained only by those branches.

Each of the first three articles of the Constitution establishes each of the three branches of government. Article I establishes the Legislative Branch, Article II establishes the Executive Branch, and Article III establishes the Judicial Branch.

In Article I, Section 1 of the Constitution the two parts of Congress, the House of Representatives and

Senate, are also established, and according to that clause, all legislative powers are granted to the two houses of Congress.

To understand the true depth of Article I, Section 1, we must examine the language used.

"Legislative powers" are the ability to make law, modify law, repeal law, and anything else that has to do with affecting law. Congress alone has the authority of legislative powers, but the laws must meet the criteria of remaining within the authorities granted "herein" the Constitution.

The Congress received its power to legislate from the States. Their authorities were "granted" by the States, meaning that the authority to make law within the authorities granted at the federal level were legally transferred from the States to the federal legislature. The grantor of powers to the federal government are the States, who hold the original authority over all powers, and gave up some of those authorities for the purpose of enabling the federal government the ability to perform its duties in the manner prescribed by the Constitution.

The word "vested" in the opening clause of the Constitution is defined as being a legal transfer of something, or in this case, an allowance to have legislative powers at the federal level; a legal transfer of some legislative powers from the State legislatures to the new Congress of the newly formed federal government.

Article I, Section 1 names the recipient of the legislative powers being granted by the States as being the Congress of the United States. Congress is the legislative branch of the federal government, and this clause indicates that not only was Congress granted all legislative powers given to the federal government, but that the branch of government consists of two houses; a Senate and House of Representatives.

The two Houses of Congress are similar to houses of other legislatures in history established in a bicameral fashion. One is an upper house, and the other is the lower house. In the Roman Republic, as well as in the British System, the upper house was one that consisted of wealthy, powerful, or noble citizens of society. The lower house was, in both cases, the House of the People. In the case of Britain, the House of Commons.

In the United States Constitution, the same dynamic was originally established. The House of Representatives is the lower house, the part of Congress closer to the people, and directly representative of the people. The U.S. Senate is the upper house, but rather than being populated by representatives of the wealthy, nobility, or the politically powerful, the Senators were appointed by the State Legislatures. Senators served the people indirectly. They were traditionally more politically savvy than their counterparts in the House of Representatives, and the primary role of the Senators was to vote in a manner consistent with what was in their State's best interest, and in a manner agreeable to the desires of the members of the State legislature.

All legislative powers at the federal level, according to Article I, Section 1, are granted to the Congress by the States for the purpose of making law, modifying law, or repealing law. The powers are "herein granted," meaning that the powers are expressly enumerated in the text of the U.S. Constitution. In other words, laws made must remain consistent with the "powers herein granted."

Article II, Section 1 uses similar language in describing that the executive power is "vested" in a President of the United States of America. The authorities "vested" in the President were "legally transferred" from the States, and the only transferred power to the executive branch is the executive power. There is no language in this clause that reveals any transfer of legislative powers, or judicial powers, to the executive branch.

Article III, Section 1 states that the "judicial Power of the United States, shall be 'vested' in one supreme Court, and in such inferior Courts as the Congress may from time to time ordain and establish." Again, the word "vested" is used, revealing that the authorities granted to the judicial branch were "legally transferred," and in this instance, those powers were transferred from the States, to the judicial branch. Article III, Section 1 states that only judicial powers were granted to the courts, not any legislative powers, nor executive powers.

Considering the language used in these clauses, the legality of certain federal functions, as applied in regards to the true definition of the separation of powers, requires a change in how our government is currently doing business. When members of the judiciary legislates from the bench, when the president issues an executive order to modify a law, or when his regulatory agencies creates law through a regulatory action, these policies or actions are in violation of the concept of the separation of powers, and are, therefore, unconstitutional. After all, "all legislative powers" were granted to the Congress, not to the judicial branch, or the executive branch. All "executive powers" were granted to the president, not to the legislative branch, or the judicial branch. All "judicial power" was granted to the courts, not to the Congress, or president. Each of their powers belong to each of the branches, and are not open to be shared, or manipulated, by other branches.

Since all legislative powers belong to the Congress, all executive powers belong to the president, and all judicial power belongs to the courts, it would be reasonable to consider that any actions by any of the branches outside their vested powers are unconstitutional. Regulations by federal departments not in line with laws made by the Congress are unconstitutional. Executive actions against an oil company such as British Petroleum (BP) regarding an oil spill, or going after banks to ensure they pay their fine for misbehaving through "predatory lending," are instances where the executive branch acted as judge, jury and executioner by determining guilt and punishment, and then carrying out those actions. Executive orders that take a legislative action by modifying existing laws are unconstitutional. Justices who, through their court rulings "legislated from the bench" are violating the concept of a separation of powers.

The concept of Separation of Powers does not stop at the relationship between the three branches of the federal government. Separation of Powers is present throughout our system of government, guiding the relationships between all parts of government.

Limited government is predicated on the foundation of providing restraints, and for the parts of government to abide by those restraints. These mechanisms are in place to control government power by dividing power as much as possible, not allowing any part of government to be its own arbiter, and to ensure checks and balances are in place at all levels to restrict any part of government from accumulating too many powers.

As a result of an extensive system of checks and balances to ensure that powers are distributed and divided in a manner that protects the individual-centric culture to function without governmental interference in relation to freedoms, natural rights, and a free market, the concept of the separation of powers goes further, and deeper, than merely the concept being applied to the three federal branches of government.

The bicameral Congress was governed by the concept of a separation of powers when the United States government was fashioned on the pages of the Constitution. Prior to 1913's Seventeenth Amendment, members of the United States Senate were appointed by the State legislatures, making the Senate the voice of the States. As the voice of the States, the U.S. Senate was a natural check against the voice of the people, the House of Representatives. No bill could be passed on to the President of the United States without first being approved by both the people (House of Representatives) and the States (Senate). Neither the people, nor the States, could take actions without the approval of the other.

After the Seventeenth Amendment became a part of the Constitution, the dynamics of our government changed. A natural check and balance between the States and the people was eliminated, and our journey towards a transitional government away from our constitutional republic accelerated.

The Separation of Powers also exists between the States, themselves. No State can overpower another. The Electoral College enables the less populous States to maintain an effective voice in presidential elections, and the fear of losing representation in the House of Representatives, should people begin to vote with their feet by moving to other States to escape less desirable States, prevents States from becoming fully tyrannical.

Too much power in any one part of any system can be dangerous, and the Founding Fathers used the concept of Separation of Powers to help protect us from centralized power, or the concentration of too much power in any part of our governmental system. By separating the powers of government, no matter how strong a particular part of government may get, when abiding by the dynamics of government established by the Constitution, no part of government has access to all powers.

CHAPTER 3

RULE OF LAW

The Rule of Law is defined as "the restriction of the arbitrary exercise of power by subordinating it to well-defined and established laws." In the Declaration of Independence, the Rule of Law is referred to as being "The Laws of Nature and of Nature's God." The principles of the American System find much of their foundation in the writings of John Locke, an English political philosopher during the 1600s, who expressed a view that government is obligated to serve the people, primarily by protecting life, liberty and property. In order for the government to be restrained enough to serve the people, the system would need to be representative, and subject to a series of checks and balances. Locke's preference was that the law, the standard on which the government system in question would need to be subordinated to, was written in the form of a constitution, and for that constitution to be guided by Divine Providence, and serve as the Law of the Land.

According to John Locke, the Rule of Law is inherent, making our rights God-given, and self-evident. The principles that stem from the laws of nature and of nature's God serve as the parameters of law, be they the authorities granted to government, or the restrictions necessary to restrain the greed for power by tyrants. Without government there is anarchy, a condition that always transitions into a tyrannical oligarchy. When there is too much government, there is too much political oppression, which also leads to a tyrannical oligarchy.

As the Founding Fathers were establishing the government in the former English Colonies, they realized that the government upon which they agreed during the Revolutionary War was too weak. The central government had no power under the Articles of Confederation, and the States naturally held all of the power. Historically, central governments concentrate all of the power at the top, forming a ruling elite that always became tyrannical and rules from the top down. What the founders were seeking was a system that located a balanced center, where a central government was formed, but restrained by the chains of the Rule of Law, as recognized by the people, and maintained through their States.

A consolidated national government was preferred by some of the men of early America, because they doubted the wisdom of establishing a representative government that gave too much power to the people. Democracies, after all, always committed suicide. A democracy, which puts all power into the hands of the people, always results in mob-rule, and ultimately, a tyrannical oligarchy.

A federal system was ultimately preferred by the majority of the delegates in attendance at the Constitutional Convention in 1787. The likelihood of the happiness and prosperity of the United States would be greater under a federal system, the supporters of federalism contended. The need was to "form a more perfect union," while protecting, preserving, and promoting the individuality and sovereignty of the various States.

The Articles of Confederation was a limited association. A national government, it was feared, would establish a supreme power that would eventually discard the Rule of Law, and instead resort to ruling in accordance to the rule of man. Under the rule of man, the laws of Nature's God would be in jeopardy, changing often based on the fickled whims of powerful men. Instead of the law existing as a strict standard, the law would be considered as being living and breathing, and able to be changed by the opinions of important politicians, or powerful judges.

The Rule of Law, as applied through a federal system, would serve as the first principle of a free and just government. John Adams explained the opinion of the Founding Fathers regarding the Rule of Law when he wrote that good government and the very definition of a republic "is an empire of laws." By requiring the leaders to enact and publish the law, and to adhere to the same law that applies to each citizen, the Rule of Law acts as a potent barrier against tyrannical and arbitrary government.

When a society exists under the Rule of Law, the system requires that the same law governs all citizens. Samuel Adams observed that the Rule of Law means that "There shall be one rule of Justice for the rich and the poor; for the favorite of the Court, and the Countryman at the Plough."

By requiring both the government and the people to adhere to the law, the Rule of Law serves as the foundational first principle for protecting our liberty.

The Anti-federalists argued that creating a federal government opened up the opportunity for tyranny. Those that defended the Constitution through speeches and essays (like the Federalist Papers) made the case that though a federal government could potentially lead to a tyrannical system, the complete lack of a federal government was an even more dangerous proposition. If the States had not united against the British Empire, the Revolutionary War would never have been won. As a nation, without a central government wielding enough power to field an army, or a central government with the power to tax in order to pay for that army, the new country would not long survive. The Articles of Confederation proved to be too weak in the face of Shays' Rebellion.

The former colonies were free and independent States. The individual-centric nature of State Sovereignty is the source of our freedom, and it was necessary that the autonomy of the States was a part of the foundation of the new government. The concepts of liberty provided for in the Declaration of Independence were obligatory, as far as the Founders were concerned, and the solid foundation of a government that protects the individual sovereignty of the States, and the citizens, must be the Rule of Law.

The concept of an individual-centric society was inherited by the Americans, based on a Saxon system of individualism based on land ownership. The Saxons in England considered themselves to be a commonwealth of freemen who existed in liberty under the auspices of the Rule of Law as defined by Nature's God. Leadership was required to make their decisions by the consent of the governed, and the laws by which the people were governed were considered to be natural laws provided by Divine dispensation.

Over time, the power became concentrated in the monarchy. The English believed power to be temporarily granted, and since nobody was above the law, the people had the right to remove rulers from their lofty positions when necessary. When the Saxon system of individual-centric government was under threat, the people put the principles of limited government in writing, producing the Magna Carta in 1215. With the principles of honest government in writing, it would be more difficult for tyrants to trample on the rights of the individual.

In 1688, the leadership of England was once again put on notice, and an ill-conceived plan to force absolute rule on the liberty-loving English was thwarted. The end result of the Glorious Revolution was the English Bill of Rights, a written charter guaranteeing God-given rights to all Englishmen.

The events in England, guided by the desire to be ruled by the Rule of Law as inspired by Divine Providence, rather than the tyrannical rule of man, set in motion the creation of the foundation for the system that would be designed during the American Constitutional Convention in 1787.

During the Revolutionary War, the patriots of the English Colonies had determined the British Empire was being ruled by despotic men, and the concept of the Rule of Law had been discarded. From the point of view of the revolutionaries, the King believed that the colonies were just another part of his realm, therefore the concept of property ownership should only be limited to a small group of land owners that had earned favor with the Crown. It was parliament's job to determine the laws and taxes under which the colonists should live under, regardless of representation. Britain claimed the colonies enjoyed virtual representation, but in the end, the King, the nobles, and the judges had complete power over making law, and imposing taxes.

The British Empire had become an oligarchy, and the consent of the governed across the Atlantic Ocean was considered irrelevant by the ruling elite in England. After the Revolutionary War, the framers of the United States Constitution understood that a nation ruled by an oligarchy of political elite is not compatible with a society that champions liberty, and individual rights. The government they aimed to create needed to be individual-centric, and one that was founded upon the concept of the Rule of Law, if it was going to protect the rights of the people, and preserve the individual ownership of property.

A nation throwing off the bonds of oligarchy, and embracing self-rule, however, did not mean that the United States would be a democracy. Though some democratic functions exist in America's mixed constitution, the United States is not a pure democracy. A democracy is a system of government ruled completely by the people. All laws and governmental functions, in such a system, are determined by the whims of the people, and their direct vote. Historically, democracies are transitional governments that, when the people seek a governmental system more efficient and stable than their fickled democracies, become oligarchies, or a governmental system characterized by the many being ruled over by a few political elites. The Founders did not desire to create a democratic governmental system. Ultimately, a democracy always breaks down, and the system that replaces it centralizes, becoming nothing more than a system like the monarchy against which the Americans had fought so hard against in order to gain independence.

The conclusion was that the United States must not be subject to the laws of men, or be subjected to the rule of men. To do so would be to open itself up to become an oligarchy. The new country needed to be a nation subject to the laws of God, governed by the Rule of Law, and have a republican form of government that features a representative system of governance. The States, and the people, hold sovereign power. The federal government is designed to be limited to authorities only necessary for protecting, preserving and promoting the union. All other authorities, specifically those authorities that would address issues directly affecting the people, is the responsibility of the States, and the local governments, where the people have more control over governmental functions.

To achieve their goal, the Founding Fathers determined that the components of the new federal government, as opposed to being a national government, would need to be one with three separate branches, whose powers are separated so that collusion between the branches would be difficult, with numerous checks and balances to ensure no part of government wields too much power, have a limitation of authorities to the federal government granted by the States, provide due process of the law with the right of a trial by jury, and be a system that ensures that the federal government does not betray the unalienable rights of the people of the United States.

The American form of government, when operating in pursuance of its Constitution, serves as a protector of the fires of liberty by preserving the union of States, and ensuring that individual freedoms and State Sovereignty maintain a voice in the system. The Rule of Law was based on God's law, and the Rule of Law was articulated in the Constitution to serve as the Supreme Law of the Land.

Not everyone supported the principles contained on the pages of the United States Constitution. The Federalists (political party), after losing the presidency, and Congress, in 1800, realized that their attempt to grow government by political means was a failure. President John Adams, in an attempt to preserve some of the power of the Federalist Party before Thomas Jefferson was able to take office, created new judicial offices, appointing as many new judges as possible. Adams' flurry of judicial appointments is historically known as "the appointment of midnight judges."

John Adams' expansion of the judiciary through the appointment of midnight judges was called by Jefferson's Democratic-Republicans "appalling." In Jefferson's view, the Federalists "retired into the judiciary as a stronghold. . . and from that battery all the works of Republicanism are to be beaten down and destroyed."

By the 1820s, the Federalists became irrelevant, and faded into history as the party became incapable of winning any elections. But, their statist dream lived on, and still does today, in a federal court system that was early on strengthened by John Marshall, the Chief Justice of the Supreme Court appointed by John Adams in 1801. The judicial branch, under Marshall, changed the face of the American System, catapulting the federal court system to the top of the political food chain through a series of court rulings that misrepresented the powers of the judiciary. These rulings, along with a series of bullying tactics from the bench, flipped the hierarchy of government, changing the dynamics of federal government, and shoving it toward tyranny through judicial fiat. Marshall was the longest serving Chief Justice in American history, giving him thirty-six years to orchestrate extensive damage to the original principles of the United States Constitution, and changing the definition of the Rule of Law.

John Marshall repeatedly reaffirmed his opinion that all federal law is supreme over all State law, and redefined "The Rule of Law" to mean the same as "The Rule of the Courts." He instructed that judicial decisions were the components that makes up the rule of law because judges were the people tasked with ruling on the law.

John Marshall redefined the American System, putting in place the mechanism that would increase the power of the courts, and alter the definition of the Rule of Law. The original intent of the States serving as the final arbiters of the Constitution was replaced by judicial review, establishing case law as the rule of law – making it based on the opinions of men, or more accurately, changing our system to one that is governed by the rule of man through a judicial oligarchy.

Figuratively speaking, once a society abandons the Rule of Law, and replaces it with the rule of men, it is not very long before they begin dancing around a golden calf.

The Founding Fathers knew that the courts were a potential danger, and in the beginning, the judicial branch was the weakest of the three branches of government. The Rule of Law is based on Nature's Law, and what the written Law of the Land is, not the wavering interpretation of the law by men seeking power. When the Rule of Law is abandoned, we become governed by the whims of culture, politicians, and judges.

"It was understood to be a rule of law that where the words of a statute admit of two constructions, the one just and the other unjust, the former is to be given them."
--Thomas Jefferson to Isaac McPherson, 1813.

"Where an excess of power prevails, property of no sort is duly respected. No man is safe in his opinions, his person, his faculties, or his possessions." -- James Madison

John Locke proposed that the rule of law was governed by Nature's Law (God's Law) and that no man, including a country's leader, or members of the judicial system, are above that law. Because the rule of law is based on natural law it cannot be interpreted, or changed, by the whims of men. To allow such latitude in the law is to have no law at all, and the society under such a system is not governed by the rule of law, but by the rule of man. When courts can make rulings as the arbiters of the law, they are not ruling based on the rule of law, but by judicial fiat.

CHAPTER 4

NULLIFICATION

Nullification is the States' right to enforce the Constitution. As the authors of the Constitution the States are essentially the parents of the federal government, and when that central government acts in a manner outside the limitations of the United States Constitution, the States may ignore the unconstitutional federal law or order on the grounds that the law or order is outside the authorities granted by the United States Constitution.

Despite the misnomer that all federal law trumps all State laws, Article VI of the U.S. Constitution is very clear that only federal laws that are within the authorities of the Constitution are the supreme law of the land.

If the federal government is the only arbiter of the Constitution, then the limits on the growth of the federal government are non-existent. The federal government could do anything it wanted by declaring such law or action to be constitutional, regardless of what the people, or the States, proclaim.

In the Virginia Resolutions of 1798, James Madison stated it was the duty of the State to interpose between the federal government and the citizens of the State.

The Kentucky Resolutions of 1798-99 were triggered by Kentucky's need to nullify unconstitutional federal laws, and in those resolutions Jefferson pointed out, "… that the general government is the exclusive judge of the extent of the powers delegated to it, stop nothing short of despotism – since the discretion of those who administer the government, and not the Constitution, would be the measure of their powers. That the several states who formed that instrument, being sovereign and independent, have the unquestionable right to judge of its infraction; and, That a nullification, by those sovereignties, of all unauthorized acts done under color of that instrument, is the rightful remedy."

Thomas Jefferson also wrote, "whensoever the general government assumes undelegated powers, its acts are unauthoritative, void, and of no force."

Madison's Report of 1800 reaffirms the Virginia Resolutions of 1798; "wherein the States must Interpose themselves between the citizens of the States and the federal government."

Today's professional politicians view the role of the federal government otherwise, believing as Joe Klein wrote in his article in *Time* magazine in February of 2012 titled "Obama's Fairness Doctrine," that the "Constitution was a stitching device, written to unify and control the States."

The false modern idea that the federal government rules over the States has forced the States to reconsider asserting their sovereignty. After over two hundred years of conditioning, the willingness to act has been met with reluctance, and the failure of both the public, and the politicians, to understand the rights of the States.

One wonders if the day comes that a State does act upon its right of nullification, will it fold like a deck chair when the federal government sues the State through their own federal court system?

State sovereignty, and the right for a State to nullify an unconstitutional law, serves as an impediment to the growth of an oppressive national central government. The separation of powers were not just among the branches of the federal government, but between the States and Washington, as well. James Madison stated that the most ardent opponents of a central government considered the

State legislatures the "sure guardians of the people's liberties" against violations from the federal government.

Our system of a divided government only functions properly when each part of that system works in line with the authorities afforded to that part of government. By the States refusing to stand up for themselves, and challenge the rapidly growing federal government, the States have relinquished their Constitutionally protected powers of restraining the federal government's quest for more power. The people, through their States, are allowing Washington to silence the States. Without the States being willing to stand up to the federal government, Washington will continue to grow unchecked, and the States will eventually become no more than powerless provinces subject to the powerful ruling authority of a tyrannical federal government.

We the People are not supposed to be powerless. A free people who fear an ever growing centralized government have the ability to stop it through their States. Nullification is an important key to restoring our constitutional republic. Without it, we become nothing more than subjects submitting to the dictates of a powerful central government. Without nullification, we will become enslaved by the federal government, squandering away the rights and freedoms of the future citizens of this nation.

In line with the final sentence of the Declaration of Independence, we must ask ourselves: Are we willing to mutually pledge to each other our lives, fortunes, and sacred honor?

Nullification begins with education. The unfortunate truth is that the concept of nullification is either feared, or misunderstood, by the politicians in our State legislatures.

Nullification is a very valuable tool, but not the only tool. Even reaching the point where the States are willing to nullify unconstitutional federal laws will require an extensive education campaign, and will require the use of other tools in our constitutional arsenal. On our tool belt, along with nullification, is a grassroots effort that includes peaceable assembly, correspondence campaigns, and a grassroots convention to audit the federal government – all of which may be necessary to bring about nullification by the States.

Nullification is a duty and obligation of the States. To understand nullification, we must understand the basic foundational nature of the Constitution. The United States Constitution is a social contract, not much unlike any other contract into which one might enter. The States wrote the contract we call the United States Constitution through their delegates, and ratified the contract, so as to create a federal government to serve the States, and deal with the external issues the States individually may not be able to handle. These "authorities" to the federal government are expressly enumerated, and the powers of the federal government are limited to those enumerated authorities.

The contract is much like a contract you may have with a construction company to add a room to your house. As the initiator of the contract, your rights regarding the contract are vast. If the construction company was to breach the contract, you have the right to reject their non-contractual actions, and to demand that they abide by the contract. The States have the same allowance (called nullification) as the originators of their contract with the federal government.

Could you imagine if you hired the construction company to add that room to your house, and then when you came back from lunch they were mowing your lawn and sweeping your walkway? "Hey," you would say, "landscaping is not in the contract."

What if they responded, "We interpreted the contract to say we can, and we are going to charge you extra for it. Arguing will serve no point, for our lawyers also say we can do as we please."

That is what is going on in today's American political

arena. The States wrote a contract with specific duties enumerated to the federal government, but in the name of "interpreting" the Constitution, the statists have decided to do things not in the contract, charge us extra for it in the form of various taxes, and then claim their lawyers (the federal court system) have confirmed they can do it and there's nothing We the People can do about it. The problem is, We the People, poisoned by a couple centuries of erroneous information (by design), have failed to recognize the unconstitutionality of the actions and laws by the federal government, and so we have failed to do anything about it.

As the writers of the contract, We the People, through our States, must be well-versed in its language of the contract, and we have the right, duty, and obligation to nullify (refuse to abide by and implement) actions and laws by the federal government that are not expressly granted to the federal government by the United States Constitution.

New authorities to the federal government can only be granted by amending the Constitution, and those proposed amendments must be ratified by at least three-quarters of the States (in other words, the federal government cannot have additional authorities unless the federal government asks the States for permission to have those authorities).

Thomas Jefferson in his draft of the Kentucky Resolutions wrote that nullification is a valuable tool, and Madison (regarding the nullification crisis) explained that when nullification is applied properly it is the State's way to "defeat the federal government's schemes of usurpation."

As the Declaration of Independence reminds us, we must have a "firm reliance on the protection of divine Providence." Nullification is a natural right, but is nothing without our loins being girt about with truth, without a breastplate of righteousness, without our feet shod with the preparation of the Gospel of peace, without the shield of faith, without the helmet of salvation, or without the sword of the Spirit, which is the word of God.

We must have the will to educate, inspire, and act; and we must be a virtuous people. If we are not a virtuous people, we are not capable of defending the United States Constitution. If we are not a virtuous people, we are not even capable of having the stomach for abiding by the standards of good government, nor the stomach to make sure our States pursue using their right of nullification against unconstitutional federal laws and actions.

CHAPTER 5

ELECTORAL COLLEGE

The Electoral College protects us from the excesses of democracy. The election of the president and vice president was never intended to be accomplished by direct election. During the era immediately following the ratification of the United States Constitution, the electors for the Electoral College (a name for the process that emerged during the early 1800s) were originally appointed by the States. The number of electors, according to Article II, Section 1 of the Constitution, is determined by the number of Representatives and Senators the State is entitled in Congress. The method used through the Electoral College is a kind of "indirect election."

After the 2000 election, where the winner of the popular vote was denied the presidency because he did not win the fight for electors, questions regarding the Electoral College arose. It was only the fourth time in history that the winner of the popular vote did not win the presidency. The other elections where the electoral winner was not the winner of the popular vote were the elections of 1888, 1876, and 1824.

The emergence of the National Popular Vote movement has threatened to eliminate the Electoral College. A number of officials in a number of States have promised to introduce legislation to abolish the Electoral College by sending the States' electoral votes to the winner of the national popular vote, regardless of how the candidate did in the State. These legislators claim that the Electoral College no longer serves a good purpose in modern politics. Ultimately, if the Electoral College is eliminated, the popular vote of the American people would determine every four years who we elect as president.

On the surface, the national popular vote argument seems reasonable. The supporters of eliminating the Electoral College say that the man receiving the most direct national popular votes should win. An indirect election such as the Electoral College, argue these folks, is simply unfair and undemocratic. In other words, they believe the American political system should operate as a direct democracy, not as the republic established by the Founding Fathers. They claim that the elimination of the Electoral College would enable the presidential election to be more in line with the "will of the people."

The Founding Fathers purposely did not make this country a democracy. The United States is a republic, equipped with checks and balances at all levels of government, including the voting process. Democracies were proven, according to the Founders, to be failures historically.

John Adams was quoted to say, "Democracy never lasts long. It soon wastes, exhausts, and murders itself. There is never a democracy that did not commit suicide."

Thomas Jefferson said, "The democracy will cease to exist when you take away from those who are willing to work and give to those who would not."

The Founders were not the only ones in history to recognize that a democracy opposed what they were trying to accomplish.

Karl Marx once said, "Democracy is the road to socialism."

Karl Marx, the father of communism, understood that the implementation of a democracy is a necessary step in the process of destroying our constitutional republic. Once the people are fooled to believe that they can receive gifts from the treasury rather than as individuals achieving their livelihood through their own self-reliance, they will continually vote in the people who ensure the entitlements continue to flow. Eventually, this mindset becomes the majority. Those that are dependent upon the government, as a group, change over time from an involved and informed electorate to a populace that lacks the understanding of the principles of liberty. As time passes, they become a class of people that are easily manipulated into believing that sacrificing individual liberty in exchange for social justice and security is a price that we must be willing to pay. Once the uninformed voters reach that point, they vote into power a tyranny, believing the propaganda that voting tyranny into office is for the common good. Eliminating the Electoral College would make it easier for these members of our society to vote into office those that promise more entitlements, because they are so blinded by their dependency upon government that they are no longer capable of recognizing the tyranny that accompanies such gifts from the treasury.

Once the majority of the voters in a democracy become the recipients of benefits from the federal government, the government achieves unchecked power, and may then violate the property rights of the productive members of society in order to provide benefits to the non-productive members of society. This is best characterized in the "tax the rich" scheme we are now seeing emerge as the rallying cry by a large number of modern day politicians.

The Founding Fathers were aware of this danger, which is why they established our system of government, and the Electoral College, in the manner they did. A true democracy becomes "mob rule," and the principles of liberty become a target for elimination.

"A democracy is nothing more than mob rule, where fifty-one percent of the people may take away the rights of the other forty-nine." -- Thomas Jefferson

In order to preserve our constitutional republic it was imperative for the vote of the people to be indirect, except when it came to voting for their representatives in the House of Representatives. The Founding Fathers divided power as much as possible, including the power of the vote.

Originally, the State legislatures appointed the electors that cast their votes in the presidential election. That changed in 1824 when all but six States decided to have the parties appoint the electors, and for the electors to vote in line with the popular vote of the State.

Originally, the U.S. Senators were appointed by the State legislatures, which ensured the voice of the States was present in the federal government. That changed in 1913 with the Seventeenth Amendment, which transferred the vote for the U.S. Senators to the popular vote.

The Founding Fathers divided the voting power as they did partially because if the power to vote for president, the House, and the Senate was all given to the people, and if the people were fooled by some political ideology that wished to destroy the republic by fundamentally changing the American System, a tyranny could be easily voted into control of all parts of the government without any checks whatsoever. When the majority of voters are uninformed in such a manner, tyranny is inevitable.

Winston Churchill understood the dangers of overly trusting an uninformed electorate with the capacity to govern, and also recognized the danger of democracies. He was quoted as saying, "The best argument against democracy is a five minute conversation with the average voter."

The elimination of the Electoral College would take away the voice of the smaller States, giving the election of the president to the seven largest metropolitan centers in the United States, and propel America even closer to becoming a democracy.

Democracy is a transitional governmental system that ultimately leads to tyranny. This was true in the days of the founding of the United States of America no less than it is true today.

"While democracy lasts it becomes more bloody than either aristocracy or monarchy…Democracy never lasts long. It soon wastes, exhausts, and murders itself. There is never a democracy that did not commit suicide." -- John Adams

"Democracy is two wolves and a sheep voting on what to have for dinner" -- James Bovard

Our country is not a democracy. Our nation was founded as a constitutionally limited republic. The indirect election of the president through the Electoral College reflects that truth, and the Electoral College is one of the last vestiges of the system of checks and balances as they apply to the voters.

CHAPTER 6

CHECKS AND BALANCES

Federalism was designed to balance the power of the national and State governments and thus limit the powers of the national government. Liberty is achieved by the proper application of the right amount of power in government.

The American System was developed with a system of checks and balances intact, a concept directly related to, and possible because of the concept of the separation of powers. With checks and balances in place, government is counterbalanced, ensuring that political power is not concentrated in the hands of any individuals or groups.

A system of checks and balances is an integral part of the make-up of a republic, and protects that republic from the dangerous expansion of a despotic government.

"When all government... shall be drawn to Washington as the center of all power, it will render powerless the checks provided of one government on another."

--Thomas Jefferson

When the Founding Fathers created the federal government through the writing of the U.S. Constitution, they realized the real danger that creating a centralized government posed. The Anti-Federalists were alarmed about the creation of a central government. They knew that tyranny always begins through a strong, central government.

Under the Articles of Confederation, the government

was too weak, and the union would not be able to withstand invasion, or insurrection, as the system stood under the Articles. So, a stronger government was needed. But, how do you create a stronger government, while simultaneously restraining it so that it does not become tyrannical against the people?

Government is a necessary evil. As James Madison said, "If men were angels, no government would be necessary." If the Founding Fathers were going to be successful in creating a limited central government, and protecting liberty in the process, they were going to need to put as many checks and balances into the system as possible. To protect the people, and the States, from the federal government someday becoming a powerful tyranny, it was necessary to install in the system various ways to stop it before the government could grow into the leviathan the anti-Federalists argued was an inevitability.

The original intent of the American System as it was designed by the United States Constitution was not for the federal government to be a powerful, unchecked centralized system. Limiting principles were put into place to protect State sovereignty, and checks and balances to ensure that too much power didn't wind up in the hands of a single branch of government, a single department, or a single individual. It was intended for Congress to debate the issues, not to just go along with what the president wanted. The States had a voice in the matter in a number of ways. Through the United States Senate the States were given "advise and consent" powers. The President needed ratification by the States through the U.S. Senate for treaties and the appointment of judges, and executive officers and officials. Even the people, through the House of Representatives served as a check and balance. The people were expected to make informed decisions on who they wanted to represent them based on the issues, not based on what entitlements they could get from the government, and those representatives would serve as a check and balance against the United States Senate, against the executive branch, and against the judiciary.

Statism, or the belief that government should be larger and stronger, and given the capability of micro-managing the lives of the citizens, was a concern by the Founding Fathers from the very beginning. Alexander Hamilton, a delegate from New York during the Constitutional Convention in 1787, and the first Secretary of the Treasury, supported the idea of a central government run by a politically elite group of rulers that had to act on every little issue for the good of the people. The purpose of the federal government, however, was not to be involved with local issues, but to only handle the external functions that exists, like providing for the common defense, handling international trade, ensuring border security, and protecting the sea routes.

Checks and Balances exist together with the concept of the Separation of Powers, enabling Congress to check the president by defunding programs, or impeaching the president (in addition to advise and consent powers). Congress can check the courts by passing legislation that nullifies or voids unconstitutional federal court rulings (Exceptions Clause, Article III). The president can check Congress by vetoing bills he believes to be unconstitutional, though Congress is capable of overriding vetoes with two-thirds vote from both Houses. States can check the federal government through nullification, and the people can check their States by voting with their feet (moving out of their State to a State that more resembles their political preferences). The people and the States can also check any other part of government by amending the Constitution, either by proposing a new amendment through Congress, or by Article V. Convention (in both cases the proposed amendments are required to be ratified by at least three-quarters of the States).

In 1787 the Founding Fathers that believed in the principles they set forth in the Constitution were considered to be radicals. They were willing to propose an extreme change towards self-governance from the accepted norm of Old World authoritarianism, where kings and dictators ruled with iron fists, without any checks against the ruling elite by the people, or any other entity.

In America, our system departed from the idea of an all-powerful monarch, granting instead the power to rule to the people through a representative government. There would be no kings, no oligarchies through government or the judiciary, and no established church with powerful clergy pulling the strings of the government or political leaders setting themselves up as the head of the church so that they could have their way with the people, nor could they rule over the people without a system of checks and balances in place. The new system was designed to ensure that even the president was not capable of acting as if he was above the law.

After more than two hundred years of liberty, however, modern day politicians are working to return the United States back to the systems that existed in the Old World, where the voices of the people, and their representatives, were disregarded, and the political leadership believed it existed above the law, and could manipulate the rule of law through political strong-arm tactics, and judicial fiat - regardless of any protest by the people to the contrary. Executive positions are being given the power to make unilateral decisions (have the final say) without any check and balance from Congress, or the people. Organizations that exist to protect our God-given rights, and Constitutional principles, are being undercut, demonized, and threatened out of existence. Our right to keep and bear arms is being maneuvered to the point that children can't even possess images of guns. The ruling elite have determined that anyone that opposes them must be bullied into compliance. Mob-rule has risen up, where groups that dare oppose the government are being identified by the media, and are being attacked by groups who support the statism we see rising in our own system.

Our American System has deteriorated into exactly the kind of tyranny the Founding Fathers warned us about, and against which they wrote the Constitution to protect us against. Statists in our governmental system scorn the Constitution, call it an antiquated document written for a long-gone era. They disregard the document, and circumvent it. Their power-grab is all that matters to them. They will continue to do more, and do worse, until they are stopped. The question is, do we have the intestinal fortitude to stand up for the Constitution, and a return to the system of checks and balances put into place by the Founding Fathers? Are we willing to take action, be it in the voting booth, through rallies, or by spreading the word about where this nation is supposed to be to other voters, and to the politicians?

The checks and balances of our system were once vast and comprehensive. Now, we have been led to believe the only check and balance that matters are the rulings of black-robed judges – and even then, we have leaders cherry-picking only the judicial opinions they agree with.

The greatest check against tyrannical government in the end is the voice of the people. The Founding Fathers were rebels. They were rebellious against tyranny. They rejected politics as usual, and recognized that it was not only their duty, but their right to "alter or to abolish" any "form of government" that "becomes destructive" to the rights and liberties of the people.

CHAPTER 7

STATE SOVEREIGNTY

The States created the federal system for the purpose of serving the States by protecting, promoting, and preserving the Union. The task was accomplished through delegates who were trusted members of their communities. During the Constitutional Convention in 1787 these delegates gathered in Philadelphia, Pennsylvania, in the same room of the same building the Declaration of Independence was debated and signed. The States, despite their autonomy and sovereignty, recognized that they were not individually fully equipped to handle the external issues that normally plagues nations, such as common defense, foreign trade, and mediation between the States whenever a dispute were to arise.

Prior to the United States Constitution, the States enjoyed complete autonomy. They were independent, individual entities that handled all issues locally. The States held "original authority" on all issues. The Tenth Amendment alludes to this reality in the language that the clause uses. It reads: "The powers not delegated to the United States by the Constitution, nor prohibited by it to the States, are reserved to the States respectively, or to the people."

Under such a system, the true power exists with the States. The States are the ultimate check and balance against the federal government, and as the authors of the United States Constitution hold the power of being the final decision-makers on what is, or is not, constitutional.

The United States is in the process of being fundamentally transformed into an oligarchy. The individuality of the States has been under attack, and the true power of government is being transferred to the courts, and a small group of powerful elites in the federal government. When the transformation is complete, the rule of law will be determined by the opinions of a few powerful men.

We the People have the duty to ensure that our governmental system does not operate outside constitutional boundaries. It is our duty to protect our God-given liberty, and restore our constitutional republic. That journey begins with understanding the original intent of the Founding Fathers, and educating ourselves and our posterity about the principles of the U.S. Constitution. Only then will our government return to the system under which it was intended to operate, namely, the rule of law. True understanding of the text of the Constitution is achieved when the student fully grasps the importance of State Sovereignty.

The United States Constitution was written to create a central government, and then limit the powers of that new federal government to only authorities necessary for it to properly function as originally intended. Protecting the sovereignty of the several States was among the primary goals of the Founding Fathers when they wrote the document. They plainly intended to strictly limit the prerogatives of the federal government to those powers explicitly assigned to it in the U.S. Constitution (Article I, Section 8 is the location of the original list of enumerated powers), while reserving to the States all other powers not explicitly prohibited to them in the document (Article I, Section 10 is one of the locations of prohibitions to the States listed in the Constitution).

American History is filled with controversy regarding the concept of States' rights. Prior to the American Civil

War one of the arguments in support of the sovereignty of the States was that a State could legally refuse to carry out federal enactments that they regarded as unconstitutional encroachments on their sovereignty, and there was nothing the federal government could do about it. This practice is known as "nullification."

Constitutional originalists of today still follow that line of thinking.

Opponents of States' rights argue that the Constitution is more of a set of guidelines that can be liberally interpreted, asserting that the federal government has "implied" powers that are not necessarily explicitly stated, but are in accord with general powers given by certain statements within the U.S. Constitution, such as the duty of the government to "provide for the general welfare."

Approaching the War Between the States, the sovereignty of the States became the primary issue that eventually led to the bloody civil war. Slavery was considered to be a minor trigger regarding the commencement of the war, and remained a minor ingredient until the Emancipation Proclamation was delivered by President Abraham Lincoln. The Emancipation Proclamation, while holding no legal powers, was actually a politically motivated move intended to back Britain off from supporting the Confederate States. By making the Civil War a noble war of the abolition of slavery, rather than simply a war over States' rights, Great Britain, who had outlawed slavery long before, bowed out quickly for fear of being criticized for siding with the slave States in a war now labeled as a war to free the slaves.

Abraham Lincoln used strategies that were not constitutional to hold together the Union, and he encroached on the rights of the southern States, which resulted in the ultimate move to ensure the sovereignty of the States, secession. He was willing to circumvent the rule of law to achieve victory, which is why among many conservative historians Lincoln is referred to as the "benevolent dictator," and the American Civil War is often referred to as "The War of Northern Aggression."

Long before the start of the War between the States, in 1831, South Carolina Senator John C. Calhoun said, "Stripped of all its covering, the naked question is, whether ours is a federal or consolidated government; a constitutional or absolute one; a government resting solidly on the basis of the sovereignty of the States, or on the unrestrained will of a majority; a form of government, as in all other unlimited ones, in which injustice, violence, and force must ultimately prevail."

Some historians contend that the War between the States was not fought to end slavery, but to centralize government. War was not used in the rest of the world to end slavery. In the Western civilized world, slavery was laid to rest peacefully in more than a dozen countries and territories without the emergence of armed conflict, during the eighteenth and nineteenth centuries. In South America there were cases of conflict in Venezuela and Columbia, but slave emancipation in those countries was used as a ruse for revolutionaries to create chaos so that they may use it to gain power in their countries.

Thomas Jefferson, in his first inaugural address, defended State Sovereignty, and the right of the States to secede. He said, "If there be any among us who would wish to dissolve this Union or to change its republican form, let them stand undisturbed as monuments of the safety with which error of opinion may be tolerated where reason is left free to combat it." He viewed the importance of State Sovereignty as being paramount, believing it to be the most important safeguard of the liberties of the people. "About to enter, fellow citizens, on the exercise of duties which comprehend everything dear and valuable to you, it is proper you should understand what I deem the essential principles of our Government, and consequently those which ought to shape its

Administration. I will compress them within the narrowest compass they will bear, stating the general principle, but not all its limitations. Equal and exact justice to all men, of whatever state or persuasion, religious or political; peace, commerce, and honest friendship with all nations, entangling alliances with none; *the support of the State governments in all their rights, as the most competent administrations for our domestic concerns and the surest bulwarks against anti-republican tendencies.*" [emphasis added]

Lincoln, and the presidents before him, brought on the American Civil War by not abiding by the constitutional concept of State Sovereignty. An abolition movement had already begun in the southern States, and though it may have taken an extra decade or so, slavery would have been abolished, most likely, without a shot ever being fired, and the deaths of over 600,000 young men. Following this line of thinking, one could say that the American Civil War was avoidable, from a slavery viewpoint, had the federal government decided not to encroach upon State Sovereignty, and force the hand of the Southern States into declaring independence through secession.

Nonetheless, the federal government exercised unconstitutional control over the States, and the American Civil War broke out. The war, however, after the British blockade was broken through the underhanded political strategy of the Emancipation Proclamation, progressed to its conclusion, ending in the defeat of the Confederacy.

In the Lincoln-Douglas Debates, Stephen Douglas accused Lincoln of desiring to "impose on the nation a uniformity of local laws and institutions and a moral homogeneity dictated by the central government."

The defeat of the Southern States in the Civil War was the end of the final attempt, and any future attempts, of States to use their sovereignty to keep the federal government under control. As the twentieth century approached, States settled into their role of servitude to the federal government, accepting the death of their sovereign power to veto or otherwise contravene enactments and policies of the federal government. It was at that point the United States ceased to be "the United States are," and became "The United States is."

In 1913 the Federal Reserve Act, implementation of the Federal Income Tax (Sixteenth Amendment), and the elimination of State representation in U.S. Congress with the passage of the Seventeenth Amendment (which changed the vote for the U.S. Senate from that of the State legislatures, to a direct vote by the people) represents, according to a number of constitutionalists, the year the federal government jumped the divide, and moved away from the Constitution's original intent more so than anytime in previous history. With the removal of the States' representation in the U.S. Government via the U.S. Senate, it seemed the only recourse States would have from there on out would be an Article V. Convention, or a direct declaration of sovereignty.

With the passage of the Federal Reserve Act, the central bankers of Europe realized that, after looking back on their own 220 years of experience with the Bank of England and other European central banks prior, American indebtedness would eventually grow so large that the central bankers would eventually own the American nation, and the federal government would be able to seize control of the populace under the guiding hand of the bankers. The concept of mercantilism would finally slam fully into place. Mercantilism, statism applied through economic manipulation, had been among the goals of past statists like Abraham Lincoln, and Alexander Hamilton.

During the first three decades of the 1900s it was difficult to determine if it was the Republicans or the Democrats who were more in favor of a strong, central federal government, and the destruction of State Sovereignty. Once Franklin Delano Roosevelt took office, ownership of a policy supporting an intrusive big federal government belonged to the Democrats. During his presidency, FDR extended federal powers far beyond what was granted to the federal government under the United States Constitution, and these dangerous policies were routinely denounced by conservative opponents of socialist legislation. Roosevelt's policies were seen as intrusive on the American people, and as obvious abridgments of States' rights.

Franklin Delano Roosevelt's successor, Harry S. Truman, continued the policy of expanding the prerogatives of the central government, ignoring the demand of a strict protection of State Sovereignty by many in his own party. The "Dixie-crats," southern Democrats that supported State's rights, left the Democratic Party and joined the Republicans. The Dixie-crats would later demand compromises in the civil rights legislation that the racists and statists of the Democratic Party were strongly against.

The Republican Party stood firmly in support of civil rights legislation. The newest members of the party, the former Dixie-crats, warned, however, that such federal legislation could be used to compromise State Sovereignty in the matter of civil rights. Democrats, meanwhile, filibustered against the Civil Rights Act of 1964 (after also opposing similar bills in 1957 and 1960), and to appease both the Democrats, and the newly Republican Dixie-crats, the bill was adjusted, and then was passed into law on July 2, 1964. In the end, it was the Republicans that were largely responsible for the enactment of Civil Rights Laws, but it was the Dixie-crats in the party that ensured the laws were written in such a way that federal intrusion on States' rights were at a minimum.

Republicans have since stood against federal entitlement programs, which also encroach upon State Sovereignty, by implementing a system of block grants to the States.

To this day, State Sovereignty continues to be under

attack. To counter those attacks, lawmakers in various States have introduced resolutions declaring State Sovereignty under the Ninth and Tenth Amendments of the U.S. Constitution. Encroachments upon State Sovereignty have been launched by the statists in the federal government through issues like gun rights, marriage, and abortion. Each time, despite the claim of State Sovereignty by the States, the federal court system has intervened and has continuously unconstitutionally ruled against State Sovereignty.

As statists continue to make moves with the intent to trample on State Sovereignty, an increased demand for States to exercise their rights, and to resist the continued federal encroachment on State and local authority, has been rising up from grassroots groups.

The potential volatility of the situation is apparent, and one may even consider it to be a possibility that there will be a showdown between State Sovereignty and federal control over the States.

CHAPTER 8

NATURAL RIGHTS

In the Declaration of Independence, the rights of the people are described as having four distinct attributes. We are *entitled* to our rights, our rights are *self-evident*, they are *unalienable*, and we are *endowed by our Creator* with these rights. According to the text of the founding document, we hold separate and equal station in society, meaning that we are individuals who are equal; and that our position as separate and equal individuals is given to us by "the Laws of Nature and of Nature's God."

A society functions best if the culture abides by a set of standards. Benjamin Franklin said that "Only a virtuous people are capable of freedom."

Godly moral standards serve as the foundation of the American System. The Judeo-Christian founding of the United States serves as an irreplaceable element in the construction of our system of liberty. A Judeo-Christian foundation has proven to be the most appropriate moral standard. According to the Founding Fathers, we have the law of morality written on our hearts. John Locke often discussed this. He called it "Natural Law." Locke's writings about Natural Law carry universal validity, both through space, and time, and were a large influence on the Founding Fathers when they constructed the American System.

According to Locke, Natural Law, and our Natural Rights, are independent things, not connected to social arrangements, conventions, or common beliefs. Our basic morals and rights are natural as opposed to artificial, meaning they are not brought about by humanity, but by the Creator. No person, or group of persons, can abolish, or amend them.

Natural Law includes rules of conduct, but these are not laws simply uttered into existence by some ruler, but are written on everyone's heart. God gave us the ability to reason our way to recognize them. Some people may refer to this self-evident knowledge of what is good and evil as being one's *conscience*.

Natural Law is the source of our moral behavior, and moral duties. Parents, for example, under the moral duties defined by Natural Law, should care for their children. This duty belongs to the parents, and therefore it means that the parents have the natural right to care for their children without interference on the part of others.

We also have natural rights that do not involve duties, such as the right to acquire property, the right to protect our property (which would also support the right to keep and bear the tools necessary for protecting said property not only from a potential criminal element, but from a tyrannical government), the right to speak freely, and the right to limit government should the political officials exceed their granted authorities. In the Declaration of Independence, the wording regarding our right to alter or abolish the government is, "That whenever any form of government becomes destructive to these ends, it is the right of the people to alter or to abolish it, and to institute a new government, laying its foundation on such principles and organizing its powers in such form, as to them shall seem most likely to effect their safety and happiness."

Natural Law, moral standards from it, and Natural Rights, are all intertwined. They are all a part of the same animal, so to speak. They are Divinely given, and are binding on us because they have been commanded by God. They are in place to provide a maximal benefit to humanity, to protect us from the consequences of immoral actions.

Our rights are God-given, therefore, it is logical to conclude that the way to determine if a moral standard, or a natural right, is indeed what it claims to be, it would need to also be sanctioned by God. In other words, God-given rights must be God-defined.

To determine if a societal or cultural whim should be categorized as a right, we must simply ask if God would sanction such a thing.

Various agendas claim to be constitutional rights, or a new civil right. Extensive lobbying campaigns, and a series of court cases, are used to convince society that not only is the target issue a constitutional right, but that it is the job of the federal government to force any and all people and States to agree with the premise, and act in a manner that supports it.

If acceptance must be compelled through the force of law, if the public must be coerced into accepting the new "right," and there is a fear that the new right interferes with the free practice of other rights, can we truly call the new right a "right"?

I have the right to swing my arms all I want, but the moment my right to swing my arms causes me to punch people who get in the way in the nose, my right to swing my arms must be adjusted, but not eliminated.

At what point does the life of a person in the womb cease to be a "right of the woman," and become a "right of the child?" When does a demand for marriage go beyond government recognition for the purpose of legal privileges that accompany civil unions, and become an infringement upon religious freedoms? Should a business be allowed to reserve the right to refuse service to anyone on religious grounds?

The premise associated with culturally motivated and government defined rights never addresses the idea regarding if government should be the "guarantor" of "constitutional rights" in the first place.

Natural Law accompanies virtue. John Adams said, "Our Constitution was made only for a moral and religious people. It is wholly inadequate to the government of any other."

Samuel Adams recognized that if we cease to be a virtuous people, and "if we are universally vicious and debauched in our manners, though the form of our Constitution carries the face of the most exalted freedom, we shall in reality be the most abject slaves."

George Washington, during his Farewell Address, said, "Of all the dispositions and habits which lead to political prosperity, Religion and morality are indispensable supports. In vain would that man claim the tribute of Patriotism who should labour to subvert these great Pillars of human happiness, these firmest props of the duties of Men and Citizens. The mere Politician, equally with the pious man, ought to respect and to cherish them... Let it simply be asked, where is the security for property, for reputation, for life, if the sense of moral and religious obligation desert the oaths which are the instruments of investigation in courts of justice?"

When one reads the Bill of Rights, a pattern emerges. In the First Amendment, it begins, "Congress shall make no law..." In the Second Amendment, the final words are "shall not be infringed." The first words of the Third Amendment read, "No Soldier shall..." In the center of the Fourth Amendment it states, "...shall not be violated."

The Bill of Rights was not originally written to enable the federal government to guarantee our rights. The language tells us that the amendments were written to tell the federal government, "hands off, do not touch," when it came to the subject of the rights of the people.

The idea that the federal government must control the States in order to ensure nobody's rights are violated at any level of government emerges in the Fourteenth Amendment.

We possess natural rights that belong to us based on the fact that we were simply born. These rights are unalienable, because they are God-given, and therefore government does not have the authority to take them away, even if in the name of protecting someone else's "government-defined" rights. It is not the government's job to guarantee our rights, either. There are no such thing as constitutional rights. Since our rights are God-given, and we are "entitled" to our "unalienable" rights, that means that we are the possessors of our rights. They belong to us, as individuals. With freedom comes responsibility, and one of those responsibilities is taking action to protect our rights. When a culture is not responsible with its rights, well-intentioned bureaucrats attempt to insert regulations, to better maintain societal balance.

When we are irresponsible with our rights, it opens the door for government to intrude upon them.

That is not a statement condoning government actions against our rights, but simply a warning because big government always takes advantage of crisis.

It is the goal of statists to change individual-centric societies into systems built upon collectivism. Group-think. A communal society where equality is not based on opportunity, or the law, but based on outcome, and the whims of powerful men.

Everybody has the right to be stupid, but unfortunately, some people abuse that privilege. As a result, things like political correctness emerge. In an attempt to be courteous, an extreme condition is met, and everyone runs around hyper-sensitive, fearing that they may offend someone. Statist systems take advantage of such crises, pitting groups against each other, inserting social engineering by manipulating language, and claiming that every want, desire, and action is a constitutional right. Individuals then take advantage of the distressed system, trying to get what they can by calling themselves victims, offended in a hurtful manner over something someone said that wouldn't have been a big deal only a decade earlier.

In addition to our rights being God-given, and therefore God-defined, in line with the reasoning that surrounds the "right to swing my arms" concept, we must also remember that sometimes there can be certain limits to our rights.

Freedom of speech, for example, is not the freedom to say whatever you want, whenever you want to. That right ceases when our speech interferes with Natural Law. One example would be slanderous speech, which is not protected by the concept that we have a right to free speech. As a result, defamation laws exist. Defamation is not free speech, and is not something that would be sanctioned by God, therefore, it is not a form of the freedom of speech.

We have a right to life. The Declaration of Independence even lists that right as one of the self-evident rights endowed by our Creator. We have a right to life, liberty, and the pursuit of happiness (property). However, a serial murderer acts in a manner that is not sanctioned by God, and in our country such a crime, once convicted, carries with it the penalty of capital punishment. Can that serial killer or rapist say, "I have a right to life?" He let go of that right when he brutally took the life of another through an action that is against natural law. The offense against God is self-evident.

What about persons who are yet to be born? Do they have a right to life? We must ask ourselves, when it comes to so-called "women's reproductive rights," would God sanction the termination of a healthy pregnancy?

In the case of marriage, we must ask, "Does a person have a *right* to marry whomever they wish?" The definition of a right, once again, is going to go back to the fact that our rights are God-given. A marriage between a man and a woman is sanctioned by God. A marriage to an animal, a person of the same sex, or a polygamous marriage, would not be.

One may argue that the commonality of polygamy in history should define it also as a "traditional" form of marriage. It was, indeed, very common in the days of the Old Testament.

The fact that something happened, and that it was noted in the Bible as a historical occurrence, does not make the action something God would sanction. We forget that most of the Bible is not doctrinal. Much of the Holy Bible is historical, making it more of a history book laying out the history of Israel. A large part of the Old Testament, and a good portion of the New Testament, is simply a record of historical events. In the Old Testament God never sanctioned polygamy, and in fact he disapproved of it, forbade it, and punished Israel for it.

Stating that something happened in history does not confirm it as being traditional, or that it should be a right. A right is a right only when it would be sanctioned by God because our rights are God-given.

The whole argument that rights are God-given, and therefore a right is not a right unless it would be sanctioned by God, may anger those who oppose a value-based society, but without that foundation of virtue, as supported by historical data, a system is doomed to collapse.

Proponents of statism understand the importance of being a godly nation, and they understand that a majority of Americans are faith-based.

With the aid of political correctness, opposing sin is being labeled by the statists as "un-Christian." Christians are labeled bigots and haters for not willfully succumbing to the demands of social engineering. Statism challenges the religious community because they are the final line of defense regarding Natural Rights, and a virtuous society. Collectivism and the demands of a socialist state cannot exist alongside a virtuous society.

The drive for statism, and the elimination of the concept of Natural Rights, are natural companions. It is a tough battle to wage. The enemy is deceptive, and alters language to create confusion and misunderstanding. They are intent upon eliminating the idea that our rights are God-given.

We must remember, as we look back upon history, that Rome fell from within. What began as a prosperous republic became a debauched society. The Romans abandoned honest government, abandoned their republic, and decayed morally within at every level.

Our Natural Rights, and the responsibilities that accompany freedom, are for us as individuals to defend. But if we are not a virtuous people that understand the foundation of the definition that is inherent to the existence of our rights, morality will become relative, and our society will collapse from within as have all other great societies that have turned their backs on the rule of law, and the Natural Rights of the people.

CHAPTER 9

SECESSION

The States are voluntary members of the Union. The States created the Union with the intention of it being a voluntary compact between the States. Peaceful secession was considered by the Founding Fathers as an essential component of the federal compact, a way to discipline the federal government should the political class running the central government seek an unconstitutional path. If membership in the Union was not considered to be voluntary, how could the compact be genuine? Voluntary membership is a key aspect of a free society. The ability to secede is a necessary part of sovereignty. If the States' membership in the Union is not voluntary, then the States are not sovereign.

Delegates of the sovereign States wrote the U.S. Constitution. If the federal government breaches the social contract called the United States Constitution, the States have a right as the originators of the contract to secede.

Alexander Hamilton, though a statist that did not appreciate the limiting principles of the United States Constitution as his colleagues did, recognized the voluntary nature of the States' membership in the Union. He proposed that the United States should be in a state of perpetual national debt, and since the States would be on the hook for their portion of that debt, they would be less likely to secede.

Hamilton knew that if the federal government would

ever have the chance to become a centralized government that controls the States, rather than a federal government that serves the States, State Sovereignty would need to be neutralized, and the concept of secession would need to be considered unlawful, and defiant. Hamilton's attack on the sovereignty of the States began early, and led to his attempt to try to rewrite history, arguing that the States had never been sovereign in the first place. As a statist, Hamilton recognized State Sovereignty as an important check and balance against the expansion of the central government. Hamilton dismissed the Jeffersonian concepts of strict constructionism, and knew that once State Sovereignty, and the threat of secession, was a forgotten footnote of history, the federal government could be unleashed to do whatever it wanted without the States standing in the way, or limiting its growth.

Nationalists like Hamilton failed to sell the idea of a leviathan government during the Constitutional Convention, and he knew he could never convince three-quarters of the States to ratify any amendment giving away their sovereignty, so he set out to manipulate the Constitution through "interpretation" and "implied law" to remold the federal government as a system of national supremacy. Through concepts like *implied powers* and *judicial review*, Hamilton's statist successors have effectively carried out his argument against a limited federal government.

Secession is a valuable tool of the States to combat statism, and to halt the advances of an ever-expanding federal government. Losing a member of the Union, in the eyes of the political class in Washington D.C., would not only represent a loss of revenue, but would be perceived as an act of defiance against the central powers. The States, as sovereign, individual, autonomous entities, entered into the constitutional contract voluntarily, and they have a right to separate themselves from that contract, if they feel it to be necessary.

Thomas Paine, in his *Rights of Man*, wrote: "The fact therefore must be that the individuals themselves, each in his own personal and sovereign right, entered into a contract with each other to produce a government: and this is the only mode in which governments have a right to arise, and the only principle on which they have a right to exist."

In Federalist 45, James Madison wrote: "The powers delegated by the proposed Constitution to the federal government are few and defined. Those which are to remain in the state governments are numerous and indefinite. The powers reserved to the several states will extend to all the objects which, in the ordinary course of affairs, concern the lives, liberties, and property of the people, and the internal order, improvement, and prosperity of the state."

John C. Calhoun, representative from South Carolina and Vice President under John Quincy Adams said: "The error is in the assumption that the General Government is a party to the constitutional compact. The States formed the compact, acting as sovereign and independent communities." Calhoun was a strong supporter of State Sovereignty, and nullification. He wrote in an essay in 1828 titled "South Carolina Exposition and Protest," arguing that States can veto any law they consider to be unconstitutional. He pushed for secession, and asserted that nullification could lead to secession, and in fact that almost happened in 1832.

In 1832 was an episode known as the "Nullification Crisis," where South Carolina challenged federal tariffs they believed to be unconstitutional. The State legislature passed a proposal nullifying them, declaring the tariffs unconstitutional. In response to South Carolina's nullification measure, Congress passed the Force Bill, empowering the President to use military power to force States to obey all federal laws. President Andrew Jackson then sent U.S. Navy warships to Charleston harbor, and

South Carolina then nullified the Force Bill, too. It all led to the Compromise Tariff of 1833, proposed by Senator Henry Clay to change the tariff law in a manner which satisfied Calhoun, who by then was in the Senate. The threat of secession was among the tools South Carolina used to ensure the federal government backed off, and returned to a more acceptable role.

John Quincy Adams also defended the right of the States to secede. In an 1839 speech he said, "The indissoluble link of union between the people of the several states of this confederated nation is, after all, not in the right, but in the heart. If the day should ever come (may Heaven avert it!) when the affections of the people of these States shall be alienated from each other; when the fraternal spirit shall give way to cold indifference, or collision of interests shall fester into hatred, the bands of political associations will not long hold together parties no longer attracted by the magnetism of conciliated interests and kindly sympathies; to part in friendship from each other, than to be held together by constraint. Then will be the time for reverting to the precedents which occurred at the formation and adoption of the Constitution, to form again a more perfect Union by dissolving that which could no longer bind, and to leave the separated parts to be reunited by the law of political gravitation to the center."

In his book, *Democracy in America*, Alexis de Tocqueville wrote, "The Union was formed by the voluntary agreement of the States; and in uniting together they have not forfeited their nationality, nor have they been reduced to the condition of one and the same people. If one of the states chooses to withdraw from the compact, it would be difficult to disprove its right of doing so, and the Federal Government would have no means of maintaining its claims directly either by force or right."

When the average American hears the word "secession," a good segment of the population will immediately think of the War Between the States. The uproar after the *Dred Scott* ruling became a focal point of the 1958 Lincoln-Douglas debates. While running for president, Abraham Lincoln famously said, "A house divided against itself cannot stand."

After Lincoln won the presidency in 1860, without even being present on the ballots in the southern States, South Carolina seceded from the Union in December. Other States seceded, and the Confederate States of America had been formed, by the time Lincoln was inaugurated on March 4, 1861. The Civil War began a little more than a month later.

After the end of the Civil War the statists immediately convened constitutional delegations to declare the ordinances of secession by the southern States in 1860 and 1861 "invalid." During the Reconstruction period, the military governors also altered the southern constitutions so that they denounced secession. Eliminating the right of secession was the federal government's way of clearing the path for the national government to stride towards centralization.

The federal courts have also participated in the effort to eliminate the right of secession. In *Texas v. White* in 1869, Supreme Court Chief Justice Salmon P. Chase wrote that, "The union between Texas and the other states was as complete, as perpetual, and as indissoluble as the union between the original states. There was no place for reconsideration or revocation, except through revolution or through consent of the States."

The case was over the Texas Ordinance of Secession. The majority opinion called the State ordinance "null," and established a narrative that rendered all acts of secession illegal according to the "perpetual union" of both the Articles of Confederation and subsequent Constitution of the United States. The statists, since the ruling, have used it exhaustively to support their argument that secession is an illegal act.

In harmony with Hamilton and Lincoln, Chase's

opinion regarding the *Texas v. White* decision suggested that the Union predated the States and grew from a common kindred spirit during the years leading to the American War for Independence. This collectivist mentality was also supported by Supreme Court Justice Joseph Story in his famous *Commentaries on the Constitution of the United States*.

Story channeled John Marshall and Alexander Hamilton in his reasoning, arguing that the Constitution was framed and ratified by the people at large, not the people of the individual States. "The constitution of a confederated republic, that is, of a national republic, formed of several states, is, or at least may be, not less an irrevocable form of government, than the constitution of a state formed and ratified by the aggregate of the several counties of the state." In his argument Story reduced the States to the status of a province, or a county.

Story defended his position with the "Supremacy Clause" in Article VI. The Supremacy Clause indicates that all laws of the United States made "in pursuance of the Constitution" are the "supreme law of the land." Story contended that correspondence sent by the Philadelphia Convention accompanying the Constitution to the State ratifying conventions was aimed at a "consolidation of the Union," arguing that the Union's existence was a collective endeavor, and one that could not be dissolved.

Those who most staunchly support the concept that secession is illegal consider it to be a traitorous act by the States. Such an argument supports the idea that the United States is a nationalistic collective, rather than a voluntary union of States in a constitutional republic.

Constitutional originalists maintain that secession remains an important constitutional tool. Even in our modern political environment, secession may be used to stave off federal statism, and preserve constitutional principles and State Sovereignty.

CHAPTER 10

FEDERAL SUPREMACY

John Marshall, the fourth Chief Justice of the United States, wrote that there is a "priority of national claims over state claims" in his opinion regarding *McCulloch v. Maryland*, 1805, which upheld an act in 1792 asserting for the United States a priority of its claims over those of the States against a debtor in bankruptcy. With subsequent opinions, Marshall, Joseph Story, and many courts since, have fostered the belief that the federal courts, and federal laws, have total supremacy over all State court rulings and laws. However, this concept contradicts the Tenth Amendment, which specifically articulates that powers not delegated to the federal government, nor prohibited to the States, belong to the States.

Not all federal laws are supreme over State laws, and the federal courts were not originally designed to be supreme over State courts when it comes to issues that fall under the sole authority of the States.

If the federal government has a law on the books, and the law was made under the authorities granted by the States in the United States Constitution, and a State, or city, passes a law that contradicts that constitutional federal law, the federal government's law is supreme based on The Supremacy Clause in Article VI. of the United States Constitution. If the federal law is unconstitutional because it was made outside of constitutional authority, it is an illegal law, and therefore it cannot be supreme over similar State laws.

An example of the federal government acting upon the assumption that all federal law is supreme over State law emerged when medical marijuana laws were passed in California. The State of California passed a law legalizing marijuana for medicinal purposes, but federal law has marijuana as being illegal in all applications. Therefore, using the authority of the federal government based on the Supremacy Clause, federal agents began raiding and shutting down medical marijuana dispensaries in California. However, there is no place in the U.S. Constitution that gives the federal government the authority to regulate drugs, nor has there been an amendment passed to grant that authority to regulate drugs to the federal government, therefore the raids on medical marijuana labs in California were unconstitutional actions by the federal government.

When the States of Washington and Colorado legalized marijuana during the Obama presidency, the federal response was different. The Obama administration refused to enforce federal drug laws, not because it would be unconstitutional to do so, but because they were trying to protect the ideological narrative of the Democrat Party. The lack of response showed that the federal government acts in accordance of the ideological narrative of the party in power before acting in accordance to the authorities granted by the U.S. Constitution.

Since the Obama administration has operated on the assumption that all federal laws are constitutional by the reality of their existence, then one could argue that the Obama administration was then guilty of unconstitutionally refusing to execute a federal law in violation of Article II, Section 3 where it states the president "shall take Care that the Laws be faithfully executed."

The Supremacy Clause, based on the text provided in

Article VI, applies only to federal laws that are constitutionally authorized. Federal drug laws are unconstitutional because there is no expressly granted authority regarding drugs listed in the Constitution. As a result, California's medical marijuana laws, and Colorado and Washington's legalization of marijuana, are constitutional because they are not contrary to any constitutionally authorized federal laws.

"Contrary" is a key word in Article VI., Clause 2. Language plays an important role in the Constitution, and the Supremacy Clause is no different. The clause indicates that State laws cannot be contrary to constitutionally authorized federal laws. For example, Article I, Section 8, Clause 4 states that it is the job of the U.S. Congress to "establish an uniform Rule of Naturalization". The word "uniform" means that the rules for naturalization must apply to all immigrants, and to all States, in the same way. If a State was to then pass a law that granted citizenship through the naturalization process in a way not consistent with federal law, the State would be guilty of violating the Supremacy Clause.

In the case of Arizona's immigration law, S.B. 1070 enacted in April of 2010, the argument by the federal government that Arizona's law is contrary to federal law was an inaccurate argument. Assuming, for just a moment, that the federal government has complete authority over immigration (which is not true since immigration is one of those issues in which the federal government and the States have concurrent jurisdiction), Arizona's law would then need to be identical to federal law. In most ways, the Arizona law is similar to federal law, save for one difference. If Arizona was to follow the federal government's recommendation, and truly pass a law completely in line with federal law, Arizona would remove its text that disallows racial profiling because the federal law does not contain such protections, which is actually the only way Arizona's law is contrary to federal law.

The language in Article VI., Clause 2 reveals clearly that only laws made under the authorities granted to the federal government have supremacy. Article VI., Clause 2 reads, "This Constitution, and the Laws of the United States which shall be made in Pursuance thereof; and all Treaties made, or which shall be made, under the Authority of the United States, shall be the supreme Law of the Land; and the Judges in every State shall be bound thereby, any Thing in the Constitution or Laws of any State to the Contrary notwithstanding."

Perhaps one of the most misunderstood and misapplied clauses of the U.S. Constitution, the Supremacy Clause has been used in line with the concept of federal supremacy. During his stint on the Supreme Court, John Jay worked feverously to establish broader powers for the courts, and to transform the federal government into a national government. He quit the Supreme Court after failing, pursuing an opportunity to be governor of New York.

Chief Justice John Marshall spent his thirty-six years on the Supreme Court attempting to establish, and expand federal supremacy, and largely succeeded. Marshall is embraced by statists as the one that successfully expanded federal supremacy in his opinion of the *McCulloch v. Maryland* case in 1819, where the Court invalidated a Maryland law that taxed all banks in the State, including a branch of Alexander Hamilton's creation, the national Bank of the United States. Marshall held that although none of the enumerated powers of Congress explicitly authorized the incorporation of the national bank, the Necessary and Proper Clause provided the basis for Congress's action. Marshall concluded that "the government of the Union, though limited in its power, is supreme within its sphere of action."

During the 1930s, under Franklin Delano Roosevelt, the Court invoked the Supremacy Clause to give the federal government broader national power. The federal government cannot involuntarily be subjected to the laws of any State, they proclaimed, and is therefore supreme in all laws and actions.

As a result of over two hundred years of misinformation the commonly accepted definition of federal supremacy is that all federal laws supersede all State laws. Often, the idea that if a federal law is unconstitutional it cannot possibly be supreme over a State law, is not even considered. . . until it is brought up as a possibility.

In other words, federal supremacy remains defined erroneously because any argument to the contrary has simply never been able to emerge through the static of misinformation.

Part Two

Unconstitutional Concepts

CHAPTER 11

IMPLIED POWERS

The United States Constitution was written to establish a federal government to handle issues the States individually could not. The States, who had original authority over all issues prior to the ratification of the United States Constitution, legally transferred some of their powers to the federal government so that it may function in the manner intended by the framers of the Constitution during the federal convention in 1787. The federal government was given express powers that are enumerated in the Constitution, but may not act upon any power not enumerated unless that action is necessary and proper to be used in order to carry out an expressly granted authority. The powers given to the federal government were carefully chosen, limiting the central government to handling only external issues that concern the Union of States, and internal issues regarding conflicts between the States, or those issues that are necessary to preserve the Union. In return, the States would be tasked with administering the remaining internal issues, specifically those affecting their own affairs.

In Federalist No. 45, James Madison explains that by design, as provided by the United States Constitution, "The powers delegated by the proposed Constitution to the federal government, are few and defined. Those which are to remain in the State governments are numerous and indefinite. The former will be exercised principally on external objects, as war, peace, negotiation, and foreign commerce; with which last the power of taxation will, for the most part, be connected. The powers reserved to the several States will extend to all the objects which, in the ordinary course of affairs, concern the lives, liberties, and properties of the people, and the internal order, improvement, and prosperity of the State."

The concept of "Implied Powers," as defined by Alexander Hamilton during his argument for a national bank, was that "there are implied, as well as express powers [in the Constitution], and that the former are as effectually delegated as the latter... Implied powers are to be considered as delegated [to the federal government] equally with express ones."

Implied Powers are assumed authorities to the federal government, according to those that support the concept, that are not expressly enumerated, but are implied based on the interpretations of the Constitution by the political class, and judges. From an early age we learn through our studies of American History as it is presented by those that oppose the limiting principles of the United States Constitution that it is the job of federal court justices to "interpret the law," which in turn leads to their authority to "interpret the Constitution."

The problem with the power of interpretation is that if you give an agency the authority to "interpret" something, their definitions will be more apt to reflect their own political ideology and agenda, than the letter of the law.

A living and breathing legal system changes at the whims of the electorate, politicians, and judges. Cultural evolution can be used to manipulate the law, changing legal definitions without using the proper tools granted by the Constitution, such as the Article V. amendment process, to get the Constitution to mean whatever the power-brokers want it to mean. The writers of the Constitution did not initiate a flimsy system that should change based on the whimsical desires of political opportunists. The American form of government under the United States Constitution was designed to be a system based on a set standard, a written foundation with specific enumerated powers expressly granted to the federal government. To allow the political elite to manipulate the Constitution based on their interpretations of the document through an unconstitutional concept they call "implied powers" is to go against the original intent of the document, to establish a direct path to tyranny, and a loss of liberty in America.

Strict constructionism recognizes that the federal government was created to serve the States, not control them. Supporters of the concept of Implied Powers suggest that the federal government can expand beyond those original restraints by simply following the opinion of a politician, or judge, regarding the constitutionality of a federal law, or action. There are powers that lie beyond what is specifically enumerated, but those powers are not "implied powers," but rather find a direct connection to authorities expressly enumerated in the Constitution in Article I, Section 8, and any subsequently enumerated authorities in other articles or sections in the Constitution, or in any amendments. Those powers are called, "Necessary and Proper."

Article I, Section 8, Clause 18, the "necessary and proper clause" (called the "Elastic Clause" by statists and nationalists) reads: "To make all law which shall be necessary and proper to carrying into execution the foregoing powers, and all other powers vested in this Constitution in the government of the United States, or in any department or officer thereof."

The language of this clause specifically establishes that only laws that may not be expressly granted as authorities, but are necessary and proper in order to carry into execution the foregoing powers, and all other powers vested in this Constitution, may be passed using this clause as their supporting authority.

Foregoing powers means "the powers expressly granted preceding this clause." All other powers vested in this Constitution means "any other powers granted by other parts of this Constitution, or by amendment."

Also notice the word "vested." Vested is defined as meaning "legally transferred." If the powers expressly given to the federal government were legally transferred, they have been transferred from someplace. Article I, Section 1 and the Tenth Amendment both explain that the original possessors of the powers granted to the federal government are the States, therefore the laws of the United States must be in accordance with those powers expressly granted, and any new powers must be obtained through the amendment process (Article V) which does not go into effect until the States ratify the request with a ratification vote of three-quarters of the States.

Any laws passed by the federal government must be in line with the expressly enumerated authorities granted by the Constitution, itself. If an authority is not specifically enumerated as a power of the federal government, it must be "necessary and proper" in order to carry out express powers granted.

As an example, in Article I, Section 8, the Constitution gives the federal government the authority to establish post offices. A necessary and proper law or federal action to carry out that express power would be if Congress purchased the land needed for the location, hired the construction company to build the facility, and hired the personnel necessary to wrap up any construction, or post-construction needs. None of those activities are necessarily granted as an authority to the federal government, but all of those activities are "necessary and proper" in order to carry out the expressly enumerated power of establishing a post office.

The government also uses the concept of "implied powers" to justify regulating companies like UPS, or Fed

Ex, because they carry out services similar to that of the post office. However, regulating those private companies is not necessary and proper in order to carry out U.S. Postal Service functions, nor is the government placing such restrictions on a private company for any reason enumerated in the Constitution. Therefore, federal regulation over private parcel delivery corporations is unconstitutional. The States, however, are not prohibited from setting rules regarding the movement of parcels within their boundaries, therefore, any regulation necessary regarding parcel delivery companies would need to be established by the States in which the companies operate.

Implied powers, according to those that support the concept, relate specifically to the legislative branch, but actually all branches have some form of implied powers.

Thomas J. DiLorenzo, in his book *Hamilton's Curse*, explains that implied powers were an invention of Alexander Hamilton, a federalist that believed in a more centralized governmental system. DiLorenzo wrote:

> Hamilton also invented the myth that the Constitution somehow grants the federal government "implied powers." "Implied powers" are powers that are not actually in the Constitution but the statists like Hamilton wish were there. As Rossiter pointed out, "One finds elaborations of this doctrine throughout his writings as Secretary of the Treasury." The most notable articulation of this idea can be found in Hamilton's Opinion on the Constitutionality of the Bank of the United States. He wrote this report in 1791, while serving as treasury secretary. President Washington had asked both Hamilton and Jefferson for their opinions on the subject. In his opinion, Hamilton wrote that "there are implied, as well as express powers [in the Constitution], and that the former are as effectually delegated as the latter" . . . He added, "Implied powers are to be considered as

delegated [to the federal government] equally with express ones." A nationalized bank, he went on to argue, was one of those implied powers.

Jefferson vehemently disagreed, arguing that the express powers delegated to the federal government in Article I, Section 8, of the Constitution (providing for the national defense, coining of money, etc.) were expressly stated because they were the only powers delegated to the federal government by the sovereign states that ratified the Constitution. Any new powers, Jefferson believed, could be delegated only by a constitutional amendment. He realized that such a doctrine as "implied powers" would essentially render the Constitution useless as a tool for limiting government if the limits of government were simply left up to the imaginations of ambitious politicians like Hamilton. . . the shock troops of the Federalist Party - federally appointed judges - would use Hamilton's arguments to essentially rewrite history and the Constitution. Thus was "liberal judicial activism" born.

. . . George Washington had condemned the notion of a "living constitution" in his Farewell Address (which, oddly enough, is said to have been at least partly ghostwritten by Hamilton). In that address President Washington said, "If in the opinion of the People, the distribution of modification of the Constitutional powers be in any particular wrong, let it be corrected by an amendment in the way the Constitution designates. But let there be no change by usurpation . . . the customary weapon by which free governments are destroyed." Hamilton's theory of implied powers ignored this warning, laying the template for generations of lawyers who would use the courts, rather than the formal amendment process, to essentially render the constitutional constraints on government null and void.

Not only were there supposedly "implied" powers in the Constitution that only the wise and lawyerly like Hamilton recognized (but that were foreign to James Madison, who like Jefferson was a strict constructionist) . . . unconstitutional powers would magically become constitutional, in Hamilton's opinion. Taken to logical ends, this argument implies that any action of the government would be de facto "constitutional" by virtue of the fact that the action occurred. This is how Hamilton viewed the Constitution - as a potential blank check for unlimited powers of government. (Thomas J. DiLorenzo, *Hamilton's Curse*, New York: Three Rivers Press, 2008, pages 26-29.)

The concept of Implied Powers is not supported by the United States Constitution. Implied Powers, along with allowing the courts to "interpret" the Constitution, and the concept of Judicial Review, have served as among the most damaging concepts used to not only circumvent and usurp the Constitution, but to destroy the principles of limited government presented by the document as originally intended by a majority of the Framers of the United States Constitution.

CHAPTER 12

JUDICIAL REVIEW

Judicial Review is a concept that says the federal court system is the final decision-maker when it comes to determining the constitutionality of laws. Laws are constantly being legally challenged regarding their constitutionality, and inevitably these challenges wind up being decided by a federal court. The common belief is that the judicial branch of the federal government is the final arbiter of the U.S. Constitution.

The problem is, there is no place in the U.S. Constitution that gives the federal court system that kind of authority.

A quick jaunt through history reveals that judicial oligarchies are not a new occurrence. The judges of the British judiciary, during the time of the American Revolution, carried nearly as much power as the king. The smug old men wore their powdered wigs arrogantly. Save for the occasional kingly correction, all rulings of the judges were final. They served the aristocracy, and suppressed dissent. The law was interpreted by these powerful judges, adjusted by their political whims, especially when it was in accordance to the tyrannical demands of the monarchy.

In the United States, the Framers of the Constitution had no desire to continue the European tradition of privileged classes. As a result of the Founders' negative opinion of elitism, the word "uniform" was used often in the U.S. Constitution. "All men are created equal" was more than just a phrase from the Declaration of Independence. It was an ultimate goal.

As with today, there were those during the era of America's founding that believed governments run best when guided by a political elite made up of educated aristocrats who have some hidden wisdom that enables them to recognize the presence of a General Will. Members of the political elite in the Colonies, and during the early years of the United States, looked up to the British system of aristocracy, mercantilism, and empire. The only obstacle between these elitists, and empire, was the Constitution, and the vote of the people - which brings us back around to the courts.

The attempt to centralize the United States government into a system reminiscent of the systems that consolidated power in Europe failed. Alexander Hamilton's Bank of the United States did not work, and the political headway achieved through Adams' presidency was all but erased when Thomas Jefferson won the presidency in the close election in 1800. Unable to achieve their statist ends through political means, Hamilton, and his fellow big government cronies, retreated to the stronghold of the judiciary, and more specifically, Chief Justice John Marshall, in order to launch their big government plans.

During John Adams' final moments in the presidency, he appointed a long list of "midnight judges." His last minute judicial appointments included sixteen Federalist circuit judges, and forty-two Federalist justices of the peace. These judges were being appointed to offices created by the Judiciary Act of 1801 (of which John Adams signed into law on February 13, 1801 – less than a month before Jefferson's inauguration) in the hopes of retaining federalist control of the courts as Jefferson's Democratic-Republicans gained control of the Congress, and Jefferson himself accepted the presidency.

While Adams was still in office, most of the commissions for these newly appointed judges were delivered. However, unable to deliver all of them before Adams' term expired, some of them were left to be delivered by the incoming Secretary of State, James Madison. Jefferson ordered them not to be delivered, and without the commissions delivered, the remaining new appointees were unable to assume the offices and duties to which they had been appointed to by Adams. In Jefferson's opinion, the undelivered commissions were void, and the judicial positions had been unlawfully created.

One of those newly appointed judges was a man named William Marbury. He sued James Madison for not delivering his commission, and the case worked its way up to the Supreme Court. After all of the dust settled, on February 24, 1803, the Court rendered a unanimous (4-0) decision that Marbury had the right to his commission. However, the court also ruled that the court did not have the power to force Madison to deliver the commission. The power of enforcement belongs to the executive branch, and it was President Jefferson that refused to give the okay to Madison to deliver the commission.

Chief Justice Marshall wrote the opinion that accompanied the ruling of the court, and in that opinion he wrote that the federal court system has the power of judicial review. Rather than simply apply the law to the cases, Marshall had decided that the courts have the authority to determine the validity of the law as well. This opinion, however, went against all of the limitations placed on the courts by the Constitution.

One of the most obvious fundamental principles of the Constitution is the limitations it places on the federal government. The Constitution is designed not to tell the federal government what it cannot do, but to offer expressly enumerated powers to which the authorities of the federal government are limited to. The powers vested in the federal government were granted by the States, and any additional authorities must also be granted by the States. The process by which this can be accomplished is through the amendment process, where it takes three-quarters of the States to ratify.

The power of Judicial Review was not granted to the courts by the States in the Constitution. The courts took that power for themselves through Justice Marshall's opinion of *Marbury v. Madison.*

When one reasons out the facts surrounding the concept of Judicial Review, we realize that the federal court system is a part of the federal government. The Constitution was designed to limit the authorities of the federal government by granting only a limited number of powers. Judicial Review enables the federal government, through the courts, to determine if the laws that the federal government made are constitutional. In other words, the federal government, through Judicial Review, can determine for itself what its own authorities are. The Supreme Court took that power for itself, and a government that takes power, or should I say "seizes" power, is a tyranny.

Do you think that is in line with the limiting principles the Founding Fathers originally set forth?

The idea that the federal courts, or the United States Supreme Court, has the authority to interpret the Constitution, and can decide if a law is constitutional or not, is unconstitutional. The concept of Judicial Review, despite its unconstitutional nature, was never stopped, and has been perpetuated by the courts in the attempt to gain power for the political elite in the federal government. Ultimately, the concept of Judicial Review works toward expanding the federal government, and making it a more centralized governmental system.

Federal judges have historically maintained that the federal courts should have the power of judicial review, or the power to determine the constitutionality of laws. In response to the judicial urgings for the powers to judge the extent of the federal government's powers, in the Kentucky and Virginia Resolutions of 1798, Thomas Jefferson and James Madison warned us that giving the federal government, through its courts, the power of judicial review would be a power that would continue to grow, regardless of elections, putting at risk the all important separation of powers, and other much-touted limits on power. The final arbiters of the Constitution are not supposed to be the courts, argued the Founding Fathers who were believers in the limiting principles of the U.S. Constitution. The power of the federal government must be checked by State governments, and the people. The States and the people are the enforcers and protectors of the U.S. Constitution.

The idea that the federal court system has the authority to interpret the Constitution, and can decide if a law is constitutional or not, is unconstitutional, and is simply an attempt by those that believe in big government to gain power, and work towards a more centralized big federal governmental system.

James Madison went into the federal convention in 1787 with opinions that were more nationalist in nature, as compared to his later opinions at the end of the convention, and afterward. His daily correspondence with Jefferson, and the volatile nature of the debates that led to the writing of the Constitution, transformed Madison. By the end of the convention, he was more of a "limited government" kind of guy.

During the early days of the convention his comments were more nationalistic, and later in the convention (and after the convention) his opinions were more in line with what the new Constitution established.

In May of 1787, at the beginning of the convention, during the first four or five weeks when little got done (they began to accomplish the task of creating the miracle that is the United States Constitution after Franklin's recommendation for prayer before each session), Madison felt the power of the State assemblies should be limited, and though he felt Congress should be the strongest branch, he also wanted to make sure there were adequate checks on Congress. Madison was not sure the courts were the best way to do that, not because of a fear of an activist court, but because he was not sure the courts would be willing to reject unconstitutional legislation.

Aside from those arguments early on, Madison said little about judicial review during the convention. Shortly after the convention, however, John Jay was sure to make mention of the practice. . . often. The federal court was established as the weakest of the three branches, and Jay wasn't sure that judicial review would ever come to be. In fact, after his governorship in New York, Jay rejected an offer by Adams to return as Chief Justice because he felt the lack of position and power of the court was "beneath a man."

Though Madison mentioned the idea of judicial review very little, early on, he did suggest that Congress be able to "negative" State laws, a kind of "congressional review" of State laws. However, since the States have original authority over every issue, and because the idea behind the Constitution was to create a federal government that served the States, rather than control the States, the idea of the federal legislature deeming State laws unconstitutional was widely rejected by the other delegates.

The debate over whether or not the federal legislature could "negative" State laws was resolved by the creation of the Supremacy Clause in Article VI., which establishes the right of the States to "negative" unconstitutional federal laws (nullification), which would be U.S. laws not made in pursuance of the United States Constitution.

Some argue that Madison suggested the existence of a power of judicial review in his Federalist No. 39 and No. 44 essays, but Madison has also, during that same time period, been quoted from conversations and letters to fear judicial review because he felt such a concept would improperly exalt judges over legislators. Personally, in my readings of Federalists 39 and 44, I don't see the "judicial review" suggestions that statists and opponents of the Constitution claim are there.

Of course, as you know, the one that really brought judicial review into the mainstream of thinking was John Marshall, in his opinion of the *Marbury v. Madison* case in 1803.

Even with Marshall's opinion in place, with the Federalists retreating to the stronghold of the courts (as Jefferson put it), judicial review really didn't kick into an out of control spiral until after the Civil War (though it did appear more often than it should have under the Marshall Court), where after the Bill of Rights being incorporated to the States (an idea by John Bingham, an Ohio representative that wrote the Equal Protection Clause) was rejected, the courts began to accomplish the "progressive" goal of incorporating the Bill of Rights to the States beginning with the Slaughterhouse Cases.

Today, we have a court system totally out of control, with judges acting as interpreters of the law rather than recognizing that the judiciary is supposed to be a system that "applies" the law. Rather than applying the law to the cases they hear, today's courts apply their opinion to the laws in question, often overriding State laws in the process.

We have to remember the original intent was not for the federal government to be the controller of the States, nor was it supposed to be the guarantor of our rights. Our rights belong to us, and they are our responsibility to maintain and protect. In fact, if you look at the language of the Bill of Rights, the original intent becomes clear.

The First Amendment begins, "Congress shall make no law. . ."

The Second Amendment ends, "Shall not be infringed."

The Third Amendment begins, "No soldier shall. . ."

The Fourth Amendment's body includes the phrase, "Shall not be violated."

In other words, the Bill of Rights does not allow the federal courts to take cases on our rights to decide if they are constitutional, and it does not call for the federal government to "guarantee" our rights. The Bill of Rights was written in a manner to tell the federal government "hands off," and "don't touch," when it comes to our rights.

Judicial Review is anchored in the idea that the government is supposed to guarantee our rights, and the federal courts are supposed to make sure the States are not stomping on those rights, but, despite Bingham's desire to incorporate the Bill of Rights to the States, laws regarding our rights are supposed to be up to the States, which is a part of government that is much closer to us than the federal government.

One final thought. A clue to show us the attitude of the Founding Fathers regarding our rights, and if the federal government should even be deciding if States are betraying our rights, exists regarding the first right enumerated in the First Amendment (freedom of religion), as indicated by Thomas Jefferson in his response to the Danbury Baptists. He told them that religion is a State issue. He told them that their plight with the Puritans had to be handled at the State level. In short, issues regarding religion were considered by Jefferson to be none of the federal government's business, and something that must be addressed at the State level. . . just like all of our other rights.

CHAPTER 13

SEPARATION OF CHURCH AND STATE

Even the textbooks in the public school system reveals that the Pilgrims first came to The New World in search of religious freedom. With this in mind, the Founding Fathers desired to protect religion from the federal government. In today's political arena, however, it seems that things have been twisted into a strange turn that proclaims that government must be protected from religion.

The first part of the First Amendment reads: "Congress shall make no law respecting an establishment of religion, or prohibiting the free exercise thereof. . ."

Why was the First Amendment written in such a manner? And where does the idea of the Separation of Church and State come in? The concept obviously does not exist in the written text of the U.S. Constitution.

To discover the origination of the idea of Separation of Church and State, one must understand the history of the colonies, and carefully read the writings of the Founding Fathers, including the series of letters between the federal government and the Danbury Baptists of Connecticut, culminating in the letters to Thomas Jefferson after he became President of the United States in 1800.

The early laws in the colonies regarding religion, The Fundamental Orders of Connecticut to which the Danbury Baptists were subject, and the series of letters from the Danbury Baptists with a final reading of the letter

Jefferson wrote to them from which the infamous concept of Separation of Church and State was eventually derived from, holds the clues to understanding the true intent of the Founding Fathers in terms of the relationship between the Church and the government.

The Founding Fathers desired that Americans be free to worship as they wished, without being compelled by government through an established religion. The key, however, is that they not only did not want the federal government compelling a person through laws to worship in a particular manner regarding religion, but that the government shall not "prohibit the free exercise thereof."

Thomas Jefferson, as indicated in his letter and his other writings, was against the government establishing a "State Church." However, he also believed that men should be free to exercise their religion as they deem fit, and that people should not be compelled to exercise religion in a manner that must follow a government mandate. A key component of the First Amendment is the phrase, "Congress shall make no law."

The Danbury Baptists were concerned over local religious freedoms, but Jefferson was clear, the federal government could not mandate anything in regards to religion. It is a State issue, and the Danbury Baptists needed to address the issue themselves. Jefferson's reference to a "wall of separation" was a proclamation that the federal government has no right to prohibit the free exercise of religion for any reason, including in the public square.

The Danbury Baptists contacted Jefferson after his electoral victory in the 1800 presidential election. Jefferson had worked with James Madison in initiating, and making into law The Virginia Act For Establishing Religious Freedom in 1786.

The text of that Act is as follows:

Well aware that Almighty God hath created the mind free;

Be it therefore enacted by the General Assembly, That no man shall be compelled to frequent or support any religious worship, place, or ministry whatsoever, nor shall be enforced, restrained, molested, or burdened in his body or goods, nor shall otherwise suffer on account of his religious opinions or belief; but that all men shall be free to profess, and by argument to maintain, their opinions in matters of religion, and that the same shall in nowise diminish, enlarge, or affect their civil capacities.

The rights hereby asserted are of the natural rights of mankind, and that if any act shall be hereafter passed to repeal the present or to narrow its operation, such act will be an infringement of natural right.

The Baptists in Danbury, Connecticut, desired a similar law to be accepted in their own State, where the established church under the Puritans treated the Baptists as second class citizens, under which Baptists were not allowed to hold political office, or even vote.

In their letter to Thomas Jefferson (October 7, 1801), the Danbury Baptist Association first congratulated Jefferson on his victory, and then asked for his help through federal means.

Sir, — Among the many millions in America and Europe who rejoice in your Election to office; we embrace the first opportunity which we have enjoyd in our collective capacity, since your Inauguration, to express our great satisfaction, in your appointment to the chief Majestracy in the United States; And though our mode of expression may be less courtly and pompious than what many others clothe their addresses with, we beg you, Sir to believe, that none are more sincere.

Our Sentiments are uniformly on the side of Religious Liberty — That Religion is at all times and places a matter between God and individuals — That no man ought to suffer in name, person, or effects on account of his religious Opinions - That the legitimate Power of civil government extends no further than to punish the man who works ill to his neighbor: But Sir our constitution of government is not specific. Our ancient charter together with the Laws made coincident therewith, were adopted on the Basis of our government, at the time of our revolution; and such had been our Laws & usages, and such still are; that Religion is considered as the first object of Legislation; and therefore what religious privileges we enjoy (as a minor part of the State) we enjoy as favors granted, and not as inalienable rights: and these favors we receive at the expense of such degrading acknowledgements, as are inconsistent with the rights of freemen. It is not to be wondered at therefore; if those, who seek after power & gain under the pretense of government & Religion should reproach their fellow men — should reproach their chief Magistrate, as an enemy of religion Law & good order because he will not, dare not assume the prerogatives of Jehovah and make Laws to govern the Kingdom of Christ.

Sir, we are sensible that the President of the United States, is not the national legislator, and also sensible that the national government cannot destroy the Laws of each State; but our hopes are strong that the sentiments of our beloved President, which have had such genial affect already, like the radiant beams of the

Sun, will shine and prevail through all these States and all the world till Hierarchy and Tyranny be destroyed from the Earth. Sir, when we reflect on your past services, and see a glow of philanthropy and good will shining forth in a course of more than thirty years we have reason to believe that America's God has raised you up to fill the chair of State out of that good will which he bears to the Millions which you preside over. May God strengthen you for the arduous task which providence & the voice of the people have cald you to sustain and support you in your Administration against all the predetermined opposition of those who wish to rise to wealth & importance on the poverty and subjection of the people

And may the Lord preserve you safe from every evil and bring you at last to his Heavenly Kingdom through Jesus Christ our Glorious Mediator.

Signed in behalf of the Association.

Nehh Dodge
Ephram Robbins The Committee
Stephen S. Nelson

Thomas Jefferson's response was cordial, yet explained to the Danbury Baptists that, even though Jefferson now held the office of the presidency, religion is not an issue that can be effected by the federal government, be it through his office, or the legislature. The following is Jefferson's final letter to the Danbury Baptists:

Jefferson's Letter to the Danbury Baptists

The Final Letter, as Sent

To messers. Nehemiah Dodge, Ephraim Robbins, &

Stephen S. Nelson, a committee of the Danbury Baptist association in the state of Connecticut.

Gentlemen

The affectionate sentiments of esteem and approbation which you are so good as to express towards me, on behalf of the Danbury Baptist association, give me the highest satisfaction. my duties dictate a faithful and zealous pursuit of the interests of my constituents, & in proportion as they are persuaded of my fidelity to those duties, the discharge of them becomes more and more pleasing.

Believing with you that religion is a matter which lies solely between Man & his God, that he owes account to none other for his faith or his worship, that the legitimate powers of government reach actions only, & not opinions, I contemplate with sovereign reverence that act of the whole American people which declared that their legislature should "make no law respecting an establishment of religion, or prohibiting the free exercise thereof," thus building a wall of separation between Church & State. Adhering to this expression of the supreme will of the nation in behalf of the rights of conscience, I shall see with sincere satisfaction the progress of those sentiments which tend to restore to man all his natural rights, convinced he has no natural right in opposition to his social duties.

I reciprocate your kind prayers for the protection & blessing of the common father and creator of man, and tender you for yourselves & your religious association, assurances of my high respect & esteem.

Th Jefferson
Jan. 1. 1802.

The Danbury Baptists, according to Jefferson's letter, were making the same mistake that the majority of the American public makes in today's political environment. The Baptists in Connecticut were seeking a governmental solution through superior political power, but the United States through its Constitution was not designed to be a nation with a strong central government dictating to the localities their own local laws. The United States, as an individual-centric country, demanded that the Danbury Baptists handle their problem locally. It was their social duty to preserve, protect, and promote their own natural rights. Religion, as with all other natural rights, exists as a God-given right, but also as something that is owned by the possessor. If one's natural rights belongs to the individual, it is the social duty of the individual to ensure that their natural rights are protected.

As much as Jefferson would have liked to assist the Danbury Baptists in their plight, in the end religion is a local issue, and religious freedom in the State of Connecticut had to be achieved by local efforts.

The Fundamental Orders of Connecticut had been adopted in 1639. Despite the protests of the Danbury Baptists, and the protests of other religious communities, the orders remained in force until the emergence of the Connecticut State Constitution in 1818.

Though the Fundamental Orders of Connecticut enabled the Puritan Church to rule Connecticut with an iron fist for so long, it also contained provisions that influenced the Constitution of the United States.

The Fundamental Orders of Connecticut contains principles indicating that government must be based on the rights of an individual. The orders spell out some of those rights, as well as how they are to be secured by the government. It provides for elections, the use of secret, paper ballots, and places limits on the powers of the government.

The individual rights in the Orders, with others added

as the years passed, remain intact in the "Declaration of Rights" in the first article of the current Connecticut State Constitution.

Early on in the United States, if there was separation of church and state to any degree, it was imposed by the clergy upon themselves. Nonetheless, America remained a very religious country, with the tenets of Judeo and Christian values intertwined in its foundation.

When Alexis de Tocqueville visited the United States in the 1830s, as a citizen of France he was likely a firm believer in the separation of church and state in a manner very similar to what we see in modern America. Based on what he had heard, he suspected what he would find in the United States was a people suffering under the "mistake" of self-governance. He believed that America would be in turmoil, struggling under the battle for power between wealthy politicians and an overly intrusive church. However, what he observed was something totally different.

In America, the politicians prayed, and the pastors preached politics, but the government restrained itself from controlling the church, and the church did not control the government. It was an environment foreign to Europeans, where monarchs and dictators battled with The Church for position, and where they often used each other to consolidate power, or establish totalitarian rule.

De Tocqueville concluded that the liberty in America, and the success of self-governance, owed its success to the virtuous nature of American society. America is great, because America is good, seems to be his conclusion in his book, "Democracy in America."

As long as the government remains restrained, and does not interfere with the Christian nature of the country, the prosperity, abundance, and liberty in America will continue. America's downfall will occur when the nation finally turns its back on God, for doing so would also mean that the American people rejects the concept that the

Blessings of Liberty, and the Natural Rights of the citizens, are God-given. When that occurs, government will proclaim itself to be the source of our rights, and individualism will give way to collectivism, and tyranny.

CHAPTER 14

DEMOCRACY

The difference between a republic, and a democracy is the same as the difference between the rule of law and the rule of man.

The word "republic" comes from the Latin "res publica," which means the 'public thing'.

Democracy comes from the Latin "demos kratein," which means the "people's rule." Pure democracy is "majority rule," or "mob-rule."

A quote often attributed to Thomas Jefferson, despite the source actually being unknown, says it in a nutshell. "A democracy is the tyranny of the majority, where 51% may take away the rights of the other 49%."

In five of his Federalist Papers essays, James Madison defines a republic, and compares its features to that of a democracy. Nationalists of the day were challenging the viability of a republic over a democracy, while other nationalists who sought a stronger central government were trying to convince the public that a difference between a republic, and a democracy, does not exist.

Madison wrote in Federalist No. 10, "A republic, by which I mean a government in which the scheme of representation takes place, opens a different prospect, and promises the cure for which we are seeking. Let us examine the points in which it varies from pure democracy, and we shall comprehend both the nature of the cure and the efficacy which it must derive from the

Union.

"The two great points of difference between a democracy and a republic are: first, the delegation of the government, in the latter, to a small number of citizens elected by the rest; secondly, the greater number of citizens, and greater sphere of country, over which the latter may be extended."

Madison wrote in Federalist No. 14, "The error which limits republican government to a narrow district has been unfolded and refuted in preceding papers. I remark here only that it seems to owe its rise and prevalence chiefly to the confounding of a republic with a democracy, applying to the former reasonings drawn from the nature of the latter. The true distinction between these forms was also adverted to on a former occasion. It is, that in a democracy, the people meet and exercise the government in person; in a republic, they assemble and administer it by their representatives and agents. A democracy, consequently, will be confined to a small spot. A republic may be extended over a large region."

Madison wrote in Federalist No. 39, "If we resort for a criterion to the different principles on which different forms of government are established, we may define a republic to be, or at least may bestow that name on, a government which derives all its powers directly or indirectly from the great body of the people, and is administered by persons holding their offices during pleasure, for a limited period, or during good behavior. It is essential to such a government that it be derived from the great body of the society, not from an inconsiderable proportion, or a favored class of it; otherwise a handful of tyrannical nobles, exercising their oppressions by a delegation of their powers, might aspire to the rank of republicans, and claim for their government the honorable title of republic. It is sufficient for such a government that the persons administering it be appointed, either directly or indirectly, by the people; and that they hold their appointments by either of the tenures just specified; otherwise every government in the United States, as well as every other popular government that has been or can be well organized or well executed, would be degraded from the republican character."

Madison wrote in Federalist No. 48, "In a government where numerous and extensive prerogatives are placed in the hands of an hereditary monarch, the executive department is very justly regarded as the source of danger, and watched with all the jealousy which a zeal for liberty ought to inspire. In a democracy, where a multitude of people exercise in person the legislative functions, and are continually exposed, by their incapacity for regular deliberation and concerted measures, to the ambitious intrigues of their executive magistrates, tyranny may well be apprehended, on some favorable emergency, to start up in the same quarter. But in a representative republic, where the executive magistracy is carefully limited; both in the extent and the duration of its power; and where the legislative power is exercised by an assembly, which is inspired, by a supposed influence over the people, with an intrepid confidence in its own strength; which is sufficiently numerous to feel all the passions which actuate a multitude, yet not so numerous as to be incapable of pursuing the objects of its passions, by means which reason prescribes; it is against the enterprising ambition of this department that the people ought to indulge all their jealousy and exhaust all their precautions."

Madison wrote in Federalist No. 51, "In republican government, the legislative authority necessarily predominates. The remedy for this inconveniency is to divide the legislature into different branches; and to render them, by different modes of election and different principles of action, as little connected with each other as the nature of their common functions and their common dependence on the society will admit. It may even be necessary to guard against dangerous encroachments by still further precautions."

Drawing from Madison's writings, it is important to understand that the Founding Fathers were not necessarily against the will of the people, but recognized that too much power in the hands of the electorate could be as dangerous as too much power in the hands of a ruling minority. A balance had to be struck. As John Adams put it, "Democracy never lasts long. It soon wastes, exhausts, and murders itself. There is never a democracy that did not commit suicide."

However, too much government opens up the opportunity for tyranny, as well. A successful republic is one that finds its foundation on a mixed constitution, a system that applies the proper amount of government. Without law there can be no freedom. With too much government there can be no freedom.

The will of the people is fine, as long as the will of the people, just like the will of the political class, remains within the limitations prescribed by the rule of law.

Democracies, in history, have always been a transitional form of government. The result of a collapsed democracy has always been the rise of an oligarchy, where a powerful few rule over the many.

When Elizabeth Powel walked up to Benjamin Franklin after the completion of the Constitutional Convention in 1787, the politically involved woman asked Franklin, "Well, Sir, what have you given us? A monarchy, or a republic?"

"A republic, Madam, if you can keep it," replied the senior statesman.

A republic.

Despite the attempt by the nationalists to convince the American people that a republic and a democracy are the same, the public rejected the concept, as well as the drive by the Federalist political party to expand the size of government. By the 1820s, the Federalist Party faded into obscurity, and for the moment, the Constitution had won.

During the 1830s, however, the lure of democracy returned.

Andrew Jackson, despite his love of the Constitution, and sound economic principles, had a flawed desire to fundamentally transform the United States from a republic, to a democracy. This is one of the reasons many Democrats view Jackson in a favorable light, and why he is considered by many to be the "father of the Democratic Party."

Jackson began what the nationalists could not. He convinced many Americans that the United Should be a democracy. The drive for democracy created confusion, and provided an opening for socialism to use the tool of democracy to begin the transformation of America.

Karl Marx recognized the usefulness of democracy as a transitional system. He once said, "Democracy is the road to socialism."

Karl Marx, the father of communism, understood that the implementation of a democracy is a necessary step in the process of destroying our Constitutional Republic. Once the people are fooled to believe that they can receive gifts from the treasury rather than achieve for their livelihood through their individual aspirations, they will continually vote in the people who ensure the entitlements continue to flow. Eventually, this mindset becomes the majority. Government dependency is a cancer that grows over time from an involved and informed electorate to a populace who lacks the understanding of the principles of liberty and can easily be manipulated into believing that sacrificing individual liberty in exchange for social justice, artificial security, and gifts from the treasury is a price that we must be willing to pay. A group dependent upon the government in such a manner, then, is primed to vote into power a potential tyranny.

Once the majority of the voters in a democracy becomes the recipient of benefits from the federal government, the government achieves unchecked power, and may then violate the property rights of the productive members of society in order to provide benefits to the non-productive members of society. This is best characterized in the "tax the rich," or "redistribution of wealth," scheme we are now seeing emerge as the rallying cry by statists in government. Samuel Adams called this method of a redistribution of wealth "schemes of leveling."

The delegates in the federal convention of 1787 were aware of the danger of collectivism, which is why they established our system of government, and the Electoral College, in the manner they did. A true democracy becomes mob rule, and the principles of liberty become a target for elimination.

Winston Churchill understood the dangers of trusting an uninformed electorate with the capacity to govern. He was quoted as saying, "The best argument against democracy is a five minute conversation with the average voter."

Democracy is a transitional governmental system that ultimately leads to tyranny, an oligarchy like socialism, fascism, or a totalitarian system. This was true in the days of the French Revolution no less than it is today.

James Bovard summed up democracy by saying that "Democracy is two wolves and a sheep voting on what to have for dinner."

My friend, Tim "Loki" Kerlin, used to say, "A republic is two wolves voting on what to have for dinner, and a well-armed sheep contesting the vote, and ensuring nobody is on the menu."

Our country is not a democracy, nor was it ever intended to be. The United States was founded as a constitutionally limited republic. The indirect election of the president through the Electoral College reflects that truth, and the Electoral College is one of the last vestiges of the system of checks and balances as they apply to the voters.

Most of the nations in the world, and throughout history, have been ruled by a powerful few. These oligarchies are most often despotic, and restrictive in terms of choice and individuality.

The "will of the people," or the "rule of the people," sounds good on the surface. Does not the U.S. Constitution begin with the words "We the People?" The Founding Fathers agreed that a government that includes an element of the vote of the people is necessary, and a good thing. However, they also understood that too much power in any one place could be dangerous. The checks and balances throughout the government as applied by the Constitution are there to ensure that no part of the government can consolidate too much power. That effort extends also to the people, and their vote, for even the people, with too much power, can misuse that power, and lead our American System towards becoming an oligarchy.

In a democracy, majority rule quickly becomes "mob-rule," where the majority begins to vote for tyrannical practices that may, for example, single out one group, or give preferential treatment to another group. Suppose the majority decides to vote away any of our natural rights, or the possessions of a particular group because that group of people has been labeled as being undesirable by propaganda, or a complicit media? Suppose the majority votes away parental rights, or through their vote outlaws possessions because they have a beef with the wealthy having more than them? In a pure democracy there is no check against the vote of the people, and once the mob realizes they can vote into place their selfish desires, or gifts from the treasury, the downward spiral of the civilization into chaos, collapse, or oligarchy is inevitable.

The rule of law is the foundation of a republic. When we discuss the rule of law, it does not mean the opinions of judges, but instead what the law actually says. In our case, the law of the land upon which the rule of law must be based upon is the United States Constitution.

In a republic, the judiciary is not authorized to rule based on their opinion of the law, but instead they are supposed to apply the law to the cases they hear. In a republic, nobody is above the law, which means that all parts of government must also adhere to the law. Government, in a republic, is limited by the law. In the American republic the Founding Fathers included other mechanisms to protect the rule of law against oligarchs, collusion, and corruption. While no system is perfect, the founders believed that the American System would be able to stand the test of time, and have the best chance to withstand the constant assault that is always a threat by those seeking power in government.

The proper application of government preserves freedom, while too much government leads to the emergence of a ruling class that limits liberty. Too little government leads the people voting into place a powerful oligarchy once the people are fooled into believing that the pure and unadulterated will of the people, and voting themselves gifts from the treasury, are in their best interest.

The word democracy does not appear anywhere in the United States Constitution, the Declaration of Independence, or in any of the State Constitutions.

Some politicians call themselves the champions of "democracy." Whenever we hear such things from a person of power, we must be aware of the agenda behind what they are saying. Those who call for democracy desire oligarchy. Those who defend our republic stands in the way of the oligarch's goal. The statists manipulate language and use deception to confuse the voter, hoping to convince him that their big government policies exist with the best interests of the population in mind.

The statists have learned well from their idols in history. They use democracy to move the population towards bondage, and political correctness to silence their opposition. Karl Marx said, "The meaning of peace is the absence of opposition to socialism."

MSNBC host Chris Matthews asked DNC chair Debbie Wasserman-Schultz what the difference between socialism and the Democrats was. She couldn't give a clear answer. In January of 2016, Mr. Matthews asked Democrat presidential candidate Hillary Clinton the same question, and like Wasserman-Schultz, Mrs. Clinton was incapable of providing a clear and definitive answer.

CHAPTER 15

LAWLESS AGENCIES

With each White House administration the opposition discusses the lawlessness of the president, and the lawlessness of the federal government under his authority. This leader is always considered lawless by those who oppose him. The last leader was considered to be lawless. And the President of the United States before him has been accused of being lawless. The reality is, every administration in the modern era has had an element of lawlessness, whether the people in power knowingly participated with that lawlessness, or not.

The executive branch was never intended to carry with it so much power. According to Article II, Section 2 of the U.S. Constitution, the president requires the "Advice and Consent of the Senate, to make Treaties," appoint "Judges to the supreme Court," and appoint all other ambassadors, public ministers and consuls, and officers of the United States Government. However, we have presidents making "agreements" with other nations without ratification by the United States Senate, making recess appointments while the Senate is not in recess, and a whole army of czars who are appointed without any oversight by Congress, and who are armed with incredible power.

Regulatory agencies, and executive branch agencies, have been making and modifying law despite the fact that Article I, Section 1 grants all legislative powers to the two Houses of Congress. In violation of the Fourth

Amendment the Internal Revenue Service (IRS) and Child Protective Services (CPS) can seize your property (or children) without due process. In the eyes of federal agencies, one is guilty until proven innocent, and fear and threats are the tools they use to ensure they receive the truth they believe to exist. While some members of the citizenry fear we may be headed towards becoming a police state, the reality is that a police state is already in place.

The U.S. Constitution was written to create the federal government, and then limit it to the role originally intended by allowing the central government only the authorities expressly granted by the Constitution. The federal government, however, over the last two hundred years, has been seizing power, expanding its scope of influence, and intimidating the States until the several States who are supposed to be sovereign entities have come to obey the powerful government in Washington, D.C., partly out of fear of reprisal, and partly out of fear of not receiving federal funding that was unconstitutionally seized in the first place.

How do you tame a lion that has experienced the taste of human flesh? How can you return evil back into the serpent? How can you unring a bell? Have we let the cat out of the bag for good? And if we have, how long before our system breaks down and returns us to a condition of bondage as suggested by Scottish historical figure Alexander Tytler?

Perhaps we are not faced with an impossible situation. As Charles R. Swindoll once said, "We are all faced with a series of great opportunities brilliantly disguised as impossible situations."

The appearance of lawless agencies in the American System, and the rash of unconstitutional practices by the federal government, are merely symptoms. Statism yearned to destroy the Constitution the moment the document was signed. Forces conspired against the concept of limited government as it was being designed during convention in 1787. There are always those that seek power, and will destroy any system that guards against the misuse of power, not necessarily because these characters seek the power for themselves, but because they believe in a system that is humanistic in nature. They place their faith not in "divine Providence," but in the fickle whims of society, and the alleged wisdom of a ruling elite.

Jean Jacques Rousseau believed in the existence of a "general will." According to Rousseau, the general will is not necessarily expressed by the people, but is presumed to be known only by the ruling elite. The general will, explained Rousseau, controls all aspects of human life, and people refusing to obey the general will must be restrained by the body politic. Rousseau's perfect system was one built upon a utopian collective in which the people are dissolved into a single unit. To achieve such a system the power structure must abolish decentralization, and remove representative institutions so that the general will may be observed and promoted by the ruling elite. The general will, according to Rousseau, was necessary for the public good.

American politicians have been following the same kind of blueprint. Their agenda is based on the philosophy that individualism cannot be trusted, so a collective must be created, and they must be the ones running the system. This is why in recent judicial cases we are seeing judges acting as if they are more interested in making a political statement than upholding the rule of law. The rule of law, which is the United States Constitution, and the Laws of Nature and of Nature's God, must be discarded for the statists to achieve their utopian collective.

To these ideologues, their agenda comes first, and the opinion of the people, even through the ballot box, means nothing to them.

As a result, the Congress and the vote of the people are becoming irrelevant, and the executive branch is gaining power in ways never intended by the Founding Fathers.

What we have is the rise of an American oligarchy, and only State Sovereignty will stop it, if the States are willing to follow through, and stick to their guns.

During the 1780s and 1790s, a Scottish political philosopher and historian by the name of Alexander Tytler suggested that lawlessness in government is inevitable, and a part of a cycle that all civilizations encounter.

The Tytler Cycle suggests that each system that achieves freedom begins in bondage. The sequence then leads the civilization, not counting bondage, through eight different conditions, before returning the civilization back to bondage. According to Tytler, the cycle lasts about two hundred to two hundred and fifty years. The sequence is a follows:

Bondage, Spiritual Faith, Courage, Liberty, Abundance, Selfishness, Complacency, Apathy, Dependence, and then back to Bondage

Tytler organized these items in a circle:

The Tytler Cycle in History

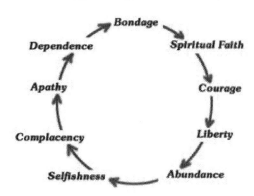

If the United States is indeed following the Tytler Cycle, then the current condition with lawless agencies, and a government that disregards the United States Constitution, is to be expected. The United States declared independence in 1776, so the time period has already exceeded two hundred years, and our system is likely somewhere between apathy and dependence.

Common sense tells us that the Tytler Cycle may very well have some validity. After all, when we look at how the first step from bondage is spiritual awakening, it makes sense. When one is in bondage, do we not cry out to God? Remember, there are no atheists in foxholes.

The Great Awakening prior to the Revolutionary War was America's move from bondage under the British Empire to spiritual faith. That faith led our Founders to be courageous, and that courage encouraged them to fight the Revolutionary War, and declare independence. The result was liberty, and in any free society, abundance (or prosperity) always follows liberty. With all of that abundance, however, it is not long before selfishness sets in, be it from expectations of success, or demands of the lower economic classes for their fair share. As their selfish desires are fulfilled, complacency and apathy becomes the norm. With their bellies full, why fight for liberty? Why care about what goes on in government? Why should anyone even notice the creeping incrementalism that is slowly changing the nature of society to one that is dependent upon the government, and ultimately one that leads the sheep back into bondage?

We accept lawless agencies and lawless actions by the federal government because we have been too satisfied to care. Our bellies are full, and politics is a problem for someone else to care about. We have too many distractions to worry about to recognize that bondage is on the horizon. When a society is filled with that much complacency and apathy, and when they have been convinced that nothing can get accomplished without the big and wonderful government there to achieve it, it is no wonder that the lawless agencies in the federal government continue to act as they do without much scrutiny, nor any protest, from the public at large.

CHAPTER 16

INCORPORATION OF THE BILL OF RIGHTS

The Bill of Rights was originally intended to be applied only to the federal government. Even the most ardent opponent to the originalist view of the Constitution concedes that it is commonly understood that originally the Bill of Rights was not intended to apply to the States whatsoever. The text of the U.S. Constitution does not necessarily clearly exhibit that the Bill of Rights was only intended to apply to the federal government, but a deep study of the text of the first ten amendments, and the various writings of the Founding Fathers on the topic, reveals without a doubt that the Bill of Rights was indeed originally intended to only apply to the federal government.

Though even the most ardent opponent of the United States Constitution will admit that the Bill of Rights was originally intended to only apply to the federal government, the rule of inapplicability to the States was abandoned by statists after 1868, when it was argued that the Fourteenth Amendment changed this rule, and served to extend most of the Bill of Rights to the States.

The section of the Fourteenth Amendment that has been interpreted to extend the Bill of Rights to the States comes from the second sentence of Section 1 of the Fourteenth Amendment, which reads:

"No State shall make or enforce any law which shall

abridge the privileges or immunities of citizens of the United States; nor shall any State deprive any person of life, liberty, or property, without due process of law; nor deny to any person within its jurisdiction the equal protection of the laws."

The assumption is that it is the federal government's job to guarantee that the States abide by that clause. In an effort to force the States into compliance, a series of court rulings has changed the Constitution by applying parts of the Bill of Rights to the States. The process over the time period since the ratification of the Fourteenth Amendment which works to apply the Bill of Rights to the States through court rulings and written opinions is called "The Incorporation of the Bill of Rights."

The Bill of Rights was originally not meant to be a guarantee of individual freedoms at all, but a limitation of federal authority against our God given rights. In other words, the Bill of Rights was not written for the people, but for the federal government as a means of telling the federal government what it cannot do in regards to our unalienable rights.

People may still ask, when faced with the puzzle regarding whether or not the Bill of Rights should be applied to the States, "Why not apply the first ten amendments to the States as well?"

The States already had a Bill of Rights in their own State Constitutions (and those that did not have a constitution yet, did include a Bill of Rights later). The Founding Fathers were confident that the people of the States could control their own State officials, and would be involved in their local governments. The people did not fear their local governments acting in a tyrannical manner similar to the potential of a centralized government system. Their fears were of the new and distant central government.

James Madison argued that a Bill of Rights was not necessary because no authorities regarding our rights were granted in the first seven articles. Alexander Hamilton agreed with Madison regarding the potential danger of including a Bill of Rights in the Constitution. Hamilton believed that articulating specific restrictions on federal power created an opportunity for power-players in government to manipulate the language and compromise the Natural Rights of the citizens. He felt it was clear that the default position of the federal government was an absence of power, and any specific power existed only by grant from the Constitution. In Federalist Paper No. 84 he argued:

> [A Bill of Rights] would contain various exceptions to powers not granted; and, on this very account, would afford a colorable pretext to claim more than were granted. For why declare that things shall not be done which there is no power to do?

Originally, parts of the first amendments proposed by James Madison and George Mason did in fact address the States, seeking to limit the State governments with provisions such as, "No state shall violate the equal rights of conscience, or the freedom of the press, or the trial by jury in criminal cases." The parts of the Bill of Rights that sought to be applied to the powers of the States, however, were not approved by Congress, and therefore were not a part of the proposed amendments to the States.

The Bill of Rights was understood, at its ratification, to be a bar on the actions of the federal government. Prior to the incorporation of the Bill of Rights to the States by the courts as based on their interpretation of the Fourteenth Amendment, the Bill of Rights did not apply to the States, and was never intended to be fully applied to the States.

The argument used, despite original intent, that the Bill of Rights must also apply to the States is based more on philosophy, than historical evidence. One of the philosophical standpoints used is that if the specific rights given in the Bill of Rights are based on the more general rights to life, liberty, and property which in turn are considered to be God-given and unalienable, then State governments do not have the authority to infringe on those rights any more than can the federal government.

The argument, however, simply *suggests* that the Bill of Rights *ought to* apply at the State level, not that it originally did.

If the Bill of Rights originally only applied to the federal government, and over time has changed to be something that was applicable on the State level through court decisions, the reality is that the Constitution itself has never allowed the Bill of Rights to be applied to the States. The change was done by judicial means, meaning that the Constitution has been changed by judicial activism. The problem, however, is that according to the Constitution, the only way to change the Constitution is through an amendment process. Therefore, the incorporation of the Bill of Rights to the States occurred unconstitutionally.

This returns us to the argument that the Fourteenth Amendment is the source and authority of the incorporation of the Bill of Rights to the States. The Supreme Court's first ruling regarding the scope of the Fourteenth Amendment, and if the amendment enables the Bill of Rights to be applied to the States, was rendered in the Slaughterhouse Cases just five years after the ratification of the Fourteenth Amendment in 1868. A five to four vote by the high court interpreted the Privileges and Immunities Clause to be the authority they needed to enforce The Bill of Rights against the States. Subsequent cases also used the Fourteenth Amendment as an authority for incorporation. During the early twentieth century a number of court cases, using the arguments referencing the Fourteenth Amendment, began selectively incorporating some of the specific provisions of the Bill of Rights while rejecting the incorporation of others.

Congressman John A. Bingham of Ohio was the

primary author of the first section of the Fourteenth Amendment, and it was his personal intention the Bill of Rights be applied to the States as well. His argument was that it was necessary in order to secure the civil rights of the newly appointed slaves. However, most of the representatives during the five months of debate on the floor of Congress argued against incorporating the Bill of Rights to the States, and so when the amendment was agreed upon for proposal, the majority of those involved intended for the Fourteenth Amendment to not influence how the Bill of Rights was applied. In the beginning, the courts ruled that the Amendment did not extend the Bill of Rights to the States. It was after the realization that Black Codes were emerging in the South that the courts decided for the purpose of protecting the civil rights of the emancipated slaves, they would begin to apply parts of the Bill of Rights to the States.

The reason why the incorporation of the Bill of Rights to the States is so dangerous is because it creates a condition that says the federal government is the guarantor of our rights. If the federal government is the guarantor of our rights, and it must force the States to comply with that concept, it not only opens Pandora's Box enabling the federal government to control the States, but it also puts the federal government in a position to be able to "define" our rights. Coupled with Judicial Review, what has emerged is a political environment where true God-given rights are being compromised (such as the right to life), while others are being redefined (such as in the case of marriage).

Part Three

Other
Concepts

CHAPTER 17

BIRTHRIGHT CITIZENSHIP

Birthright citizenship is an issue that accompanies the immigration issue. The question that brings the concept of birthright citizenship to the surface is the question over whether or not anchor babies are automatically citizens because they were born on American soil. The question regarding birthright citizenship hinges on the proper interpretation of the Citizenship Clause at the beginning of the Fourteenth Amendment.

The language of the Citizenship Clause was carefully crafted because the writers wanted it to remain in line with the original intent of the Founding Fathers, especially when it came to the dangers of divided allegiance.

The Citizenship Clause is the first clause of the Fourteenth Amendment, and it was intended to ensure that the children of the emancipated slaves, as well as the newly freed slaves, would be considered citizens without any room for argument.

The clause reads: "All persons born or naturalized in the United States and subject to the jurisdiction thereof, are citizens of the United States and of the State wherein they reside."

The misinterpretation of the clause we encounter in today's political environment exists partly because of agenda, and partly because we have been convinced to believe the clause reads, "all persons born in the United States are automatically citizens."

The defining term in the clause that enables the reader

to recognize that citizenship needs more than just being born on American soil is the part of the clause that reads: "and subject to the jurisdiction, thereof."

The word "and" comes after the part that says "All persons born or naturalized in the United States." The word "and" immediately reveals that there is more to citizenship than merely being born in American territory. This is not to say that persons born outside the United States cannot be citizens. The Immigration and Naturalization Act of 1790, and its successor in 1795 clearly clarifies the intent in regards to citizenship of American children born outside the United States. Both acts place an emphasis on protecting the country from divided allegiance, of which the writers of the Citizenship Clause of the Fourteenth Amendment recognized, while still bestowing citizenship to children of American citizens, with a few caveats.

Another argument used by those that wish to rewrite the Constitution by redefining its terms is that the word "jurisdiction" in the Fourteenth Amendment means, "the limits or territory within which authority may be exercised," which is indeed one of the definitions of "jurisdiction" in today's language. Using that definition, one can see the opposition's argument, because that would make any baby born inside the limits of the United States an American citizen.

Constitutional definitions, however, are not based on the whims of an ever-changing lexicon, but the original definitions intended as agreed upon during the final ratification process. What this means is we must ask ourselves what was meant back in 1866.

To understand "and subject to the jurisdiction, thereof," one must go to the debates recorded in the *Congressional Globe*, which is the congressional record of the Fourteenth Amendment congressional debates. In those debates the intent of the language of the amendment, "and subject to the jurisdiction, thereof" was meant to mean "full allegiance to America."

Remember, the Founding Fathers faced the danger of loyalists to the British Empire in their midst. They were adamant about protecting the fledgling country against persons with divided loyalties.

The writers of the Fourteenth Amendment wished to follow the importance of "full loyalty" as portrayed by the Founding Fathers. As far as the Founders were concerned, there could be no divided allegiances. They expected citizens to be fully American.

Despite the defeat of the Confederacy in the War Between the States, after hostilities ended the emancipated slaves were not receiving the rights and privileges of American citizens as they should have been. The former slaves were present in the United States "legally," and because they were here legally they were "subject to the jurisdiction, thereof," but they were still not receiving any assurance of equal protection under the law.

The Civil Rights Act of 1866 was created in the hopes of correcting the problem. Some of the language in the Civil Rights Act of 1866 states, "All persons born in the United States, and not subject to any foreign power, excluding Indians not taxed, are hereby declared to be citizens of the United States. ... All persons within the jurisdiction of the United States shall have the same right in every State and Territory to make and enforce contracts, to sue, be parties, give evidence, and to the full and equal benefit of all laws and proceedings for the security of persons and property as is enjoyed by white citizens, and shall be subject to like punishment, pains, penalties, taxes, licenses, and exactions of every kind, and to no other."

The definition of "persons within the jurisdiction of the United States" in that act was: "all persons at the time of its passage, born in the United States, including all slaves and their offspring, but not having any allegiances to any foreign government."

Michigan Senator Jacob Howard, one of two principal

authors of Section 1 of the Fourteenth Amendment (the Citizenship Clause), noted that its provision, "subject to the jurisdiction thereof," excluded American Indians who had tribal nationalities, and "persons born in the United States who are foreigners, aliens, who belong to the families of ambassadors or foreign ministers."

Exact quotes:

Mr. HOWARD: I now move to take up House joint resolution No. 127.

The motion was agreed to; and the Senate, as in Committee of the Whole, resumed the consideration of the joint resolution (H.R. No. 127) proposing an amendment to the Constitution of the United States.

The first amendment is to section one, declaring that all "persons born in the United States and Subject to the jurisdiction thereof, are citizens of the United States and of the States wherein they reside. I do not propose to say anything on that subject except that the question of citizenship has been fully discussed in this body as not to need any further elucidation, in my opinion. This amendment which I have offered is simply declaratory of what I regard as the law of the land already, that every person born within the limits of the United States, and subject to their jurisdiction, is by virtue of natural law and national law a citizen of the United States. This will not, of course, include persons born in the United States who are foreigners, aliens, who belong to the families of ambassadors or foreign ministers accredited to the Government of the United States, but will include every other class of persons. It settles the great question of citizenship and removes all doubt as to what persons are or are not citizens of the United States. This has long been a great desideratum in the jurisprudence and legislation of this country."

He even went out of his way to indicate that children born on American soil of foreign citizens are not included.

Clearly, the framers of the Fourteenth Amendmenthad no intention of freely giving away American citizenship to just anyone simply because they may have been born on American soil.

The second author of the Citizenship Clause, Illinois Senator Lyman Trumbull, added that "subject to the jurisdiction of the United States" meant "not owing allegiance to anybody else."

The full quote by Senator Trumbull reads:

"The provision is, that 'all persons born in the United States, and subject to the jurisdiction thereof, are citizens.' That means 'subject to the complete jurisdiction thereof.' What do we mean by 'complete jurisdiction thereof?' Not owing allegiance to anybody else. That is what it means."

Trumbull continues, "Can you sue a Navajo Indian in court? Are they in any sense subject to the complete jurisdiction of the United States? By no means. We make treaties with them, and therefore they are not subject to our jurisdiction. If they were, we wouldn't make treaties with them...It is only those persons who come completely within our jurisdiction, who are subject to our laws, that we think of making citizens; and there can be no objection to the proposition that such persons should be citizens."

Senator Howard concurred with what Mr. Trumbull had to say:

Mr. HOWARD: "I concur entirely with the

honorable Senator from Illinois [Trumbull], in holding that the word 'jurisdiction,' as here employed, ought to be construed so as to imply a full and complete jurisdiction on the part of the United States, whether exercised by Congress, by the executive, or by the judicial department; that is to say, the same jurisdiction in extent and quality as applies to every citizen of the United States now."

Based on these explanations by the writers of the clause, then, it is understood that the intention was for those who are not born to American citizens to have no birthright to citizenship just because they simply were born inside the borders of this country.

The courts have interpreted the Citizenship Clause to mean other things, but we must remember that the Constitution cannot be changed by the courts. Changes to the Constitution can only be made by amendment.

The Fourteenth Amendment's Citizenship Clause does not need to be repealed as some politicians may suggest. It simply needs to be followed in accordance to its original intent. Anchor babies are born to parents who do not have full allegiance to the United States, and are therefore not automatically citizens of America just because their birth occurred on American soil.

CHAPTER 18

EXECUTIVE ORDERS

George Washington issued eight executive orders during the entirety of both terms of his presidency. Presidents Adams, Jefferson, Madison and Monroe issued a grand total of seven executive orders among the four of them. John Quincy Adams issued three. President Andrew Jackson was the first to reach double digits, with twelve. Ulysses S. Grant was the first President to issue over a hundred, issuing 217 executive orders during his time in office. Theodore Roosevelt, Woodrow Wilson, and Calvin Coolidge each issued more than a thousand apiece, with Wilson's total of 1,803 far surpassing the other two. Franklin Delano Roosevelt signed 3,721 executive orders, surpassing each president in history, including recent office holders. Since Truman's 907 executive orders, and Eisenhower's 484, no President has surpassed 400 official executive orders. Of the remaining modern day Presidents, Ronald Reagan leads the pack with 381. [http://www.presidency.ucsb.edu/data/orders.php]

Among Mr. Washington's most well-known executive orders was the Thanksgiving Proclamation. Abraham Lincoln's most famous executive order was the Emancipation Proclamation. Executive orders are nothing new, and are perfectly constitutional, as long as they remain within the authorities granted to the federal government, and within the authorities granted to the executive branch.

Executive orders are supposed to be either proclamations, or written instructions for the purpose of altering procedures or rules concerning the operations of the executive branch. Presidents, however, have often used them for other, unconstitutional reasons.

Article I, Section 1 of the United States Constitution provides that all legislative powers shall be vested in a Congress. Any executive orders written with the intent to create, modify, repeal, or refuse to enforce the law (In violation of Article II, Section 3) are unconstitutional, and therefore illegal.

Many of the executive orders by Calvin Coolidge and Ronald Reagan were for the purpose of repealing unconstitutional executive orders by previous presidents who held a view of the American System that was less in line with the vision of the Founding Fathers.

Under criticism for his excessive use of executive orders, and more specifically his unconstitutional use of executive orders to modify legislation, President Barack Obama shifted his strategy and began to issue executive memos (once called "letters") and verbal executive actions ("pen and a phone") which are customarily unnumbered. As a result, the official number of executive orders issued by President Obama is less than that of any President of the United States since John F. Kennedy, aside from President Ford, despite the fact that in reality, Obama's total likely exceeds that of any President of the United States in history.

Keeping track of executive orders has become more organized with the passage of time. Giving each executive order a number began in 1907, with the Department of State assigning numbers to all orders in their files dating from 1862. With the effort to number the executive orders in place, and as the program expanded, the frequency of unnumbered orders declined sharply.

The Federal Register Act in 1936 provided the opportunity for the numbering and documentation of executive orders to be even more thorough. Unnumbered executive orders prior to 1936 were assigned a number already in use together with an associated letter following the assigned number.

Current practices require that all numbered executive orders are published, though under the Federal Register Act not all orders need to be published if they have "no general applicability and legal effect." Occasionally, the text of some orders is not available, as a result.

The true total of unnumbered orders is unknown. Estimates have reportedly ranged as high as fifty thousand. Executive orders that have unconstitutional legal effect are assumed to have increased with the passage of time, but the distinction between numbered and unnumbered orders, and the subject matter, general applicability, public interest, or legal effect they influence is unclear.

President Barack Obama's executive orders are not the only orders to come under scrutiny in modern politics. President Bill Clinton's executive orders and land proclamations were responded to by Congress with hearings and the consideration of several bills designed to curb the president's authority to issue such directives. The federal court system even went so far as to strike down one of President Clinton's executive orders. [http://www.heritage.org/research/reports/2001/02/the-use-and-abuse-of-executive-orders-and-other-presidential-directives]

With all of the attention executive orders receive, the sad reality is that public understanding regarding the proper use of these presidential decrees is infinitesimal. Public attention has generally been minimal. What people do not understand does not anger them. When people are exposed to the reality of the abuse of executive orders as a result of media attention, governmental messaging is often quick to steer the public away from the issue, and the distractions of surviving in an ever-changing economy usually keeps the public's attention on the matter short-lived.

When it comes to recognizing whether or not an executive order is constitutional, the concept of separation of powers is a good place to start.

The inclusion of separation of power principles in the United States Constitution is largely the result of the Framer's studies of the writings of Montesquieu. The French political philosopher, while agreeing with historical figures like Polybius that a mixed constitution was necessary to secure liberty, also recommended separating the different parts of government in order to guard against collusion between the branches. In parliamentary systems, the executive is a part of the legislative branch. In the Roman Republic, the consuls (executive branch) and orators (judicial branch) were also members of the legislature. According to Montesquieu, in order to stand the test of time, a government designed to secure liberty must be established with the different parts of government remaining separate from each other, and with their respective powers vested only to them. Collusion between the parts of government, according to Montesquieu, would destine the system to become a tyranny.

The discussion regarding the use of separation of powers principles fill the pages of James Madison's notes of the 1787 Federal Convention, the Federalist Papers, and the records of the debates during the State ratification conventions following the signing of the United States Constitution. The concept of separation of powers is established and provided for in the first sentences of each of the first three articles of the U.S. Constitution.

President Bill Clinton, and President Barack Obama, have verbalized that their use of the executive power of executive orders were used when the attempt to achieve a legislative objective failed. In other words, executive orders were used by Clinton and Obama for the purpose of achieving their agenda, despite a contrary vote in Congress. In the case of Clinton, he also repeatedly flaunted his executive order power to curry favor with narrow or partisan special interests. Clinton's top White House political advisers even made public statements about his use of executive decrees that were designed to incite a partisan response.

While it would be a mistake to try to restrict a President's lawful and proper executive order authority, Congressional failure to limit an abusive president who issues unlawful executive orders is a sign of cowardice, and that the Congress is complicit in the president's pursuit of more power, especially when Congress has the authority to curb such presidential activities.

Supporters of executive orders that exceed the powers conferred upon the executive branch by the United States Constitution argue that precedent establishes authority. According to their reasoning, if a president got away with an unconstitutional executive order in the past, the action became constitutional because no attempt to stop the order's enforcement was successful. In the case of Clinton, he also used claims of implied and inherent authority.

The president's powers do extend to taking "care that the laws be faithfully executed." Executive orders may be used regarding the ability of an agency to properly execute federal law. However, these agencies may only execute existing law, and may not create, modify, or repeal any federal law. As indicated earlier, all legislative powers belong to Congress.

When the president, or any of the agencies or officers within the executive branch, are lawfully exercising their functions, written directives may be used to ensure those functions are properly performed. How the executive power may be exercised may be specified by Congress, and when that happens, the executive branch is required to remain within those limitations. For example, a specification prohibiting certain persons from immigrating into the United States may be a part of a particular immigration law. As long as that prohibition is on the books, agencies under the executive branch must abide by that specification as they execute immigration law.

President Abraham Lincoln tended to use presidential directives unconstitutionally during the War Between the States, warning Congress that they must either adopt his directives as legislation, or he would cut off support for the Union army. On April 15, 1861, Mr. Lincoln issued a proclamation activating troops, as well as issuing executive orders to procure warships and to expand the size of the military. The directives also provided for payment to be advanced from the Treasury without congressional approval. Congress acquiesced because of the wartime circumstances, and Lincoln's actions were never challenged in court.

President Franklin Roosevelt greatly expanded the use of executive orders, in part to facilitate the expansion of governmental powers domestically, and partly to better enable him to perform as Commander in Chief during World War II without congressional interference. As did Lincoln, FDR made it a habit to abuse his executive order authority, establishing executive powers that are not expressly enumerated in the Constitution. President Harry Truman followed this pattern of governing by executive order, often acting on his own without congressional oversight or confirmation.

The Supreme Court struck down Truman's "Steel Seizure Case," calling his action "questionable when there is no grant of constitutional authority to him (express or inherent) and his action is contrary to a statute or provision of the Constitution."

Truman's desegregation of the military forces, though an admirable action on the surface, was also acted upon without congressional approval. While the president has the constitutional authority to act as Commander in Chief, which gives him the authority to assign individual soldiers lawfully in his command to units that he deems appropriate, only Congress retains the authority to create or abolish the military forces, and "make Rules for the Government and regulation" of the military. The Uniform Code of Military Justice is Congress's established standards for the armed forces.

The argument that supports Truman's desegregation of the armed forces (Remember, the original decision to segregate the military was made by Truman's fellow Democrat, Woodrow Wilson) claims that Congress's unwillingness to desegregate the military violated other provisions of the Constitution, so Truman was not interfering with any congressional power, but was instead ensuring that the constitutional provisions against racial discrimination were being properly executed.

Presidents since Truman generally remained within their constitutional and statutory grants of authority in the exercise of their executive order authority, until the Administration of President Clinton. The number of illegal executive orders issued by President Clinton consists of less than half of his total. However, the pattern of illegal orders, often without any claim of statutory or constitutional authority, were flagrant.

When Clinton wrote an executive order with the intent to force employers to be unable to replace striking employees with non-union personnel, the court ruling regarding the striker replacement case led to a decision that proposed the president may not use his statutory discretion in one area to override a right or duty established in another law.

While President Clinton's illegal executive orders were written with the intent to further improper policy or political objectives, many of President Bush's early executive orders were written to rescind or revise the illegal executive orders of his predecessors.

The problem is that these executive orders, if not rescinded, are considered to be precedent by future administrations. In today's society it is commonly believed, despite the original intent of the Constitution, that calling forth the militia (and therefore proclaiming martial law) is something that may be accomplished by executive order. Despite the fact that there are no authorities granted to the president to allow him to declare martial law or call forth the militia, the belief that these are indeed executive authorities stems from Abraham Lincoln directing much of the early Civil War by proclamation, including calling forth the militia. President Lincoln issued executive orders for the purpose of calling forth the militia and establishing martial law, and because there were never any successful challenges to his unconstitutional directives, future presidents have assumed they have the same power based on the precedent established by Lincoln.

Signing Statements are executive orders that often sneak under the wire. A presidential "signing statement" is a written statement attached to a bill when the president signs it into law. Presidential signing statements may identify a provision of the bill that the president believes is unconstitutional, or a provision he is in disagreement with, and through the signing statement he instructs executive branch officials not to enforce the provision. Though modern Presidents believe they have this power, the proper action would be to veto the entire bill due to the "unconstitutional provision," or due to the disagreeable provision, and then ask Congress to rewrite the law without the provision in question included. A signing statement ordering all executive branch officials not to enforce a particular provision in the statute violates Article I, Section 1 of the U.S. Constitution where it states that all legislative powers are vested in Congress. The president may not legally make modifications to a bill, but he may recommend a modification to a bill. If a modification is made by a House of Congress as a result of his recommendation, it still requires both Houses of Congress to approve the change.

Executive orders are generally reviewed by the

Attorney General, or another senior official in the Department of Justice, to review the directive with regard to form and legality. Since the Attorney General is a part of the executive branch, that is like a fox asking another fox if the security measures in the hen house meet their standards.

There are some directives that may remain secret, and are not made available to the general public. These include many military and national security orders. These orders are still required to be within the legal authorities granted to the president by the U.S. Constitution.

While executive orders may serve as a valuable tool for the President of the United States to use, in the end the reality of the concept of separation of powers, and the fact that in Article I, Section 1 of the Constitution all legislative powers are granted to Congress, restricts the scope of executive powers. Any executive order that creates, modifies, or repeals law is unconstitutional. There are no legal authorities offered by the Constitution that gives the president any legislative powers.

.

CHAPTER 19

ORIGINAL AUTHORITY

State Sovereignty is the key to understanding Original Authority, and Original Authority is the key to understanding the United States Constitution. The original thirteen States, as colonies, developed independently as individual, unique, and autonomous entities. In the same way that people are unique individuals, so were the colonies, and so were the thirteen original States.

Each of the States developed their own cultures, languages, and way to go about their business. In some States, established churches were heavily involved in the political scene, while in Rhode Island there was no established church, and in Pennsylvania the Quaker majority did not require one to be a Quaker in order to vote, or hold office. While cities and industry emerged in the northern States, the rural character of the South was maintained well into the nineteenth century, even after the Revolutionary War and the ratification of the U.S. Constitution. The people did not consider themselves to be Americans as much as they were residents, and citizens, of their States.

The attitude of sovereign autonomy carried into their membership of the Union. As a result, retaining the sovereignty of the States as individual and autonomous entities was very important to early Americans. Each of the States held all governmental authorities prior to the writing of the United States Constitution. Under the

149

Articles of Confederation, the central governmental organization held little power over issues. Localism remained strong, important, and something the citizens of each State were willing to take up arms to defend. All governmental powers belonged to each of the States, and those authorities were retained by the States, much in the same manner that each country that is a member of the European Union retains all of their individual authorities. As sovereign States, the delegates of the States during the 1787 Constitutional Convention sought to retain original authority as much as possible, while granting to the new federal government the few powers necessary to carry out the functions the federal government would be expected to have in order to carry out the functions it was intended to carry out.

Anti-Federalists feared the new government. In history, tyranny has always emerged through centralized government systems. And, historically, when a government becomes a tyranny, the process of includes a betrayal of the God-given rights of the people. Therefore, the Anti-Federalists demanded, after the signing of the Constitution, that the States not ratify the document unless promised a Bill of Rights. The crowning finality of that Bill of Rights addition to the Constitution is the Tenth Amendment, which serves as the last vestige of Original Authority in the Constitution.

The Tenth Amendment states that all authorities not granted to the federal government, and not prohibited to the States, are "*reserved* to the States respectively, or to the people."

The word "reserved" was used, in the context of the U.S. Constitution, for the purpose of enabling the States to "retain for future use" the authorities they already possessed prior to the writing of the Constitution. The States granted some of their authorities to the federal government so that it may properly function as designed, but they retained those authorities they did not choose to give to the federal government, and those authorities they chose not to prohibit from themselves. They were able to "reserve" those powers because they held them originally in the first place.

As the federal government has expanded, and the creeping incrementalism of statism has engulfed the American System, among the targets for destruction by the growing central government has been Original Authority. The voice of the States has been diminished over the last couple centuries, through Judicial Review, Incorporation of the Bill of Rights to the States, removing the States' voice from the U.S. Senate through the Seventeenth Amendment, removing the States' voice from taxation through the Sixteenth Amendment, attacks on the Electoral College, and through federal controls against the States in the name of civil rights. As a result, Original Authority is but a shell of its original form. The individualism and autonomy of the States has been reduced to a mere formality, and what is left of Original Authority continues to come under attack by the statists. Rather than use tools like nullification, or the Article V. Convention, the battered States seek constitutional correction through the federal courts.

Seeking help against federal tyranny through the federal courts, which are comprised of federal judges who are paid by federal funding by the federal power-brokers in the upper echelon of the federal government usually doesn't work out well for the States.

Restoration of the constitutional republic, as is sought by groups like the Tea Party, Libertarians, and various constitutionalists will not, and cannot, be achieved without a return to Original Authority. Without the sovereignty of the States being reestablished, and without the States seeking to restore their role as the final arbiters of the United States Constitution, the battle against tyranny is a futile endeavor. Only through a restoration of Original Authority can, and will, the Constitution be reestablished as the law of the land, and will the rule of law return as the governing force in the United States of America.

Statists recognize that Original Authority is the key to destroying the Constitution. This is why their attacks continue to hammer upon the remaining remnants of the individualism of the States. Tyranny seeks to control the States, and make them uniform in all ways. To destroy Original Authority completely is to finally destroy liberty.

CHAPTER 20

CIVIL RIGHTS

The issue of Civil Rights is a sticky one. While few are generally against the granting of Civil Rights to groups who are considered "wronged," or "oppressed," supporters of expanding the scope and powers of the federal government have used the concept of Civil Rights as a tool to encourage and nurture other concepts such as nationalism, statism, and Judicial Review. Through bureaucratic processes and judicial fiat the very character of Civil Rights has been altered. Issues that can be exploited in a manner that benefits the statist agenda are being redefined as Civil Rights. Though the end goal is bondage, the statists shroud their efforts with labels that proclaim freedom. Through the efforts of the statists the very concept of freedom itself has been redefined to mean "do whatever you want despite any standard of virtues or morality." In turn, common sense, and common virtue, have been compromised, replaced by concepts like political correctness, hate crime laws, secular humanism, "alternative lifestyles," and #blacklivesmatter.

Slavery served as the starting point for the agenda. There is no doubt that slavery was among the great sins in American and world history. The emancipation of the slaves was an inevitability, thank God, though I am not so sure "war" was necessary to achieve it. While the abolition of slavery was a good thing, and a necessary eventuality in the advancement of any society, through the good deed of abolishing slavery, the seeds of federal supremacy, and the death of State Sovereignty, were watered and nurtured. Historical figures like Alexander Hamilton and John Marshall had already planted the seeds, but men like Abraham Lincoln and Thaddeus Stevens ensured that those growing tendrils of authoritarianism germinated.

In tune with the federal government's denial of State Sovereignty and the death of localism, the federal government proceeded to occupy the southern States, and use military force to compel them into compliance. The federal government created a legal system that proclaimed it was designed to protect the Civil Rights of those who were once in slavery, and the leaders in Washington D.C. were willing to use military force to ensure the southern States complied.

The South's refusal to change with the times was confirmed by their new State constitutions, and various State laws, that maintained segregation, and inequality. In the minds of the statists of the time-period, and historians that look back upon that period, the South's refusal to behave necessitated federal government intrusion into State matters in order to ensure that the Civil Rights of the former slaves were maintained. It was a trying time in American history, both for a people seeking freedom after centuries of forced servitude, and for the limiting principles of the United States Constitution the Framers so carefully crafted in 1787.

The concept of Separation of Powers, especially as it pertains to the concept's application between the federal government and the States, was being reinvented. While the concept was originally designed to prevent one person, or part of the government, from becoming too strong, the federal government has used the principle of Separation of Powers to send a message to the States that they have no business interfering with the work the federal government is achieving in the name of "the common good."

The battle regarding a Separation of Powers has been waged constantly on the battlefield of Civil Rights. Shortly after the American Civil War, after the assassination of Abraham Lincoln, Tennessee Democrat Andrew Johnson, Lincoln's vice president, succeeded to the presidency.

Johnson took the oath of office on April 15, 1865. The readmission of the southern rebel States into the Union remained to be accomplished, and the manner in which that readmission should take place was a highly disputed issue. The Civil Rights of the newly emancipated slaves was a part of Johnson's great conundrum. Should the former Confederate States be readmitted? And if so, after the readmission, what rights should the freedmen, or ex-slaves, have?

Johnson's execution of his plan for reconstructing the South commenced immediately after he took the oath for President of the United States. Johnson pardoned all rebels except Confederate leaders, restored all rebel property except for slaves, and he authorized each rebel State to call a convention of white delegates to draw up a new State Constitution. Once a new State constitution was written, and approved, a new State government could then be formed, and the State could apply for readmission to the Union.

Each and every one of the new State constitutions disallowed blacks to vote in their States. President Johnson had no problem with the idea of not allowing the former slaves to vote.

Johnson's comment regarding the refusal of the southern States to allow the emancipated slaves to vote was that if Blacks were allowed to vote in the South, "It would breed a war of races."

The United States Congress was dominated by the Republicans in both Houses. The legislators were outraged by Johnson's approval of what was going on in the South. The Republicans saw the same men who had led the rebellion returning to power throughout the South, and knew that nothing good could come of it. As a result, "black codes" were being passed. These laws that were contradictory to the Civil Rights of the former slaves would add to the difficulties for blacks to work in certain jobs, own land, or even quit his job with a white employer.

An even greater concern was that President Johnson was continuing Lincoln's lead of acting through executive fiat despite congressional concerns, or legislation. The power being used by President Johnson had allowed the president, on his own authority, to establish a reconstruction plan for the South despite the protests of the members of Congress. Republicans believed establishing a reconstruction plan was the job of Congress, and Congress alone.

The Republican Congress passed the Freedmen's Bureau Bill in February of 1866. The new proposed law called for the distribution of land to the newly emancipated slaves, provided schools for their children, and set up military courts in southern States to protect the Civil Rights of blacks in the South. President Johnson vetoed the bill, calling it unconstitutional and too expensive. The Republicans failed to garner enough votes to override his veto.

Johnson accused the Republicans in Congress of being "new rebels" who were plotting to take over the federal government. He charged that Congress was acting in a traitorous manner in a vein similar to that of Jefferson Davis, the Confederate leader. "Give us the names!" a voice in the crowd shouted. Johnson named three Republican leaders of Congress as being a part of the rebellion, and in response the Republicans in Congress began to unite in their opposition to Johnson, calling him "King Andy."

In March of 1866 Congress passed the first Civil Rights bill. The proposed law declared the former slaves to be U.S. citizens and gave them the right to make contracts, sue, be witnesses in court, and own land. Johnson vetoed the bill, claiming it would "operate in favor of the colored and against the white race." The Republicans overrode his veto by a two-thirds majority in both the House and Senate, marking the first time in American history that Congress had achieved the overturning of a presidential veto.

The Republican majority in Congress, though united in their opposition to Johnson, failed to find a single reconstruction plan for the South upon which they agreed. Some Republicans supported Johnson's program, while others sought a more conservative way to readmit the former Confederate States. Some desired that the southern States should be treated as "conquered provinces." Despite the disagreements regarding reconstruction, the Civil Rights of blacks remained at the center of each of the discussions.

An elder statesman, Thaddeus Stevens, had his own radical ideas regarding Reconstruction. The member of the House of Representatives from Pennsylvania believed the rebel States were no longer a part of the Union, and had illegally removed themselves from the social contract known as the United States Constitution, and therefore, they should be treated as if they were U.S. territories. As punishment for bringing about the War Between the States, Stevens suggested that the federal government should confiscate the property of these traitors to the Union, and give the land to the newly freed Blacks (forty acres for each adult male). According to Stevens, this would break the back of the old slave-holding class and prevent it from regaining political power in the South.

Stevens, and the supporters of his plan to protect the Civil Rights of the former slaves, began as a minority in Congress, but they gained steam after Stevens successfully worked to build a coalition of House members and senators to deal with all Reconstruction matters. The Joint Committee on Reconstruction consisted of nine representatives and six senators, most of them hand-picked by Stevens. Through his committee, Stevens created a powerful voice in determining congressional action on Reconstruction. President Johnson called the Joint Committee the "French Directory," a reference to the dictatorship by committee that emerged during the French Revolution.

Congress, continuing to buck against Johnson, passed a constitutional amendment that would become the Fourteenth Amendment. The amendment begins with a Citizenship Clause, with the intent to establish without any argument that the newly emancipated slaves were all citizens of the United States. The Fourteenth Amendment also sought to prohibit the southern States from depriving any and all citizens of "equal protection of the laws." Thus began the long and difficult road to establish the Civil Rights of blacks.

The president has no say when it comes to the proposition of amendments, so Johnson could do nothing but condemn the proposed Fourteenth Amendment.

The Civil Rights movement for the former slaves was then kicked up a notch during the summer of 1866, when a group of whites and blacks attempted to hold a political convention in New Orleans. A mob of ex-Confederate soldiers attacked the convention members. The New Orleans police not only failed to protect them, but actually joined in the attack. Nearly forty convention members, mostly black men, were killed. The "New Orleans massacre" shocked northerners, and solidified the idea that the federal government must take control of the southern States, to ensure that the former Confederates ceased to misbehave.

Though no southern State ratified the Fourteenth Amendment on its first try, the northern States strongly supported it. Congress then passed a Reconstruction law much stronger than Johnson's weak plan. It was described at the time as being "written with a steel pen made out of a bayonet." The law abolished all southern State governments set up under Johnson's program, and replaced them with five military districts, each commanded by an army officer. Martial law was authorized, and the occupation of the South by the federal government, with federal troops and military courts, began. President Johnson vetoed the law, saying that it would create an "absolute despotism" over the South, but Congress promptly overrode his veto.

Later laws by Congress required each southern State to hold new constitutional conventions, but this time the delegations were required to be made up of both white and black delegates. The new State constitutions were required, by Congress, to include the right to vote for all black adult males. Then, Congress directed the southern States to ratify the Fourteenth Amendment before they would be allowed to apply for readmission to the Union. Johnson vetoed every one of the laws Congress was passing, and each and every time Congress overrode his veto.

After establishing their own Reconstruction Laws, Congress turned to President Johnson. In an effort to get the runaway executive under control, the Republicans passed the Tenure of Office Act, which prohibited the President from firing any appointed government official, even his own cabinet members, without Senate approval.

Johnson claimed the act violated the Constitution's concept of Separation of Powers, and vetoed the Tenure in Office Act as an unconstitutional invasion of his executive power. Congress, however, overturned his veto.

In 1868, after President Johnson attempted to fire his Secretary of War, Edwin Stanton, without Senate approval for assisting Congress in undermining his reconstruction policies, the House of Representatives filed articles of impeachment.

According to those seeking to impeach Johnson, the president refused to cooperate or compromise over the Civil Rights of blacks, and the Reconstruction of the South.

The impeachment trial in the U.S. Senate lasted over a

month, and after it was all over, the Senate failed by one vote to convict Johnson and remove him from office.

Despite the failure to remove Johnson, military occupation of the South remained, and Johnson had only about nine months left in his term.

The Fourteenth Amendment, in the name of Civil Rights, enabled the federal government, following the end of Johnson's presidency, to strengthen its power against the States. In the minds of those supporting the expansion of federal control over the States, it was all for the common good. The States in the South could not be trusted to be fair to blacks, and therefore, the federal government would need to force the southern States to behave.

As a result of the assault on State Sovereignty, power-brokers seeking to expand the scope and power of the federal government have taken advantage of the opportunities afforded by the concept of Civil Rights.

Natural Rights could easily be compromised in the name of Civil Rights. Anything considered a Civil Right receives special consideration, a kind of "preferential" treatment. Any group seeking to become a "protected minority" under the perceived benevolent hand of an all-powerful federal government must only convince the culture, and political class, that they too are simply seeking their own place-setting at the Civil Rights table.

As a result of federal intrusion, and newly emerging federal definitions, the enumerated rights in the Bill of Rights are at risk.

The First Amendment was written to prohibit Congress from passing laws that would infringe upon the Natural Rights of religion, speech, the press, assembly (association) and the right to petition the government for a redress of grievances.

In the name of Civil Rights, however, some groups have succeeded in convincing the federal government to limit these Natural Rights. To speak out against the attempt to compromise our First Amendment rights is seen as being a "phobia," and through laws designed to ensure "peace and safety," federal judges are allowing indefinite detention of Americans without due process if they are seen by the courts as being persons who are compromising the Civil Rights of other politically-favored persons.

On the books are laws that allow the Secret Service to arrest anyone protesting near the president (or other designated officials), laws that allow mass spying by federal agencies, and now the federal government has discovered that in order to carry out authoritarian tyranny, they only need to be the definers of what is a Civil Right, and who is considered to be a potential domestic terrorist.

Through the federal government the same agencies that have the power to define what is, or is not, a Civil Right, also are the ones who are given the power to keep surveillance on Americans, and to choose who may be detained without due process.

Gun control and gun rights advocates have no qualm with Civil Rights issues in general, but have a tendency to be reviled by federal intrusion into State matters. These supporters of the Second Amendment, more often than not, stand against the federal practice of making up its own Civil Rights definitions.

As a result, those who support an expansion of the scope and power of the federal government view gun owners as the opposition, and fail to recognize gun ownership as an individual right.

The emerging conventional wisdom is that Civil Rights trumps all other rights. If something is labeled as a Civil Right, no religion has a right to believe in a manner that opposes the federal government's definitions of what is a Civil Right. Any speech or press that opposes the federal government's definition of a particular Civil Right is considered to be "hate speech." Any assembly of persons for the purpose of opposing the federal government's definition of a Civil Right is considered to be seditious. Private businesses who refuse to serve any person protected by the federal government's definition of a Civil Right can be punished by federal law for daring to stand against that definition. Any petition, law or State constitutional amendment opposing the federal government's definition of a Civil Right will be struck down in federal court. Those who seek to arm themselves to protect themselves against the rising authoritarianism of the federal government are considered to be potential domestic terrorists, and any federal intrusion into that person's life is considered reasonable, and necessary, for the common good, and the protection of the Civil Rights of others as defined by the federal government. Failure to comply will result in the citizen being defined as either a radical extremist, or a sufferer of a mental health issue – thus, nullifying that person's right to keep and bear arms, and voiding any other associated privileges, in the eyes of the federal government.

As a result, the other amendments in the Bill of Rights are also under assault. We no longer feel secure in our persons, houses, papers, and effects, against unreasonable searches and seizures. Law enforcement agencies are going too far with lockdowns and involuntary door-to-door searches. The federal government has long abandoned any attempt to refrain from depriving people of life, liberty, or property, without due process of law. Property is being taken for private purposes, or in the name of "environmental conservation." It is becoming more common for the federal government to prosecute cases based upon "secret evidence" that they don't show to the defendant, or sometimes even the judge hearing the case. The government uses "secret evidence" to spy on Americans, and to prosecute Americans for leaking information, or for terrorism charges. And through the rising system of government tyranny through new definitions of Civil Rights for groups that have voiced that their desire to destroy the American System, federal government officials and prosecutors are using the legal system to crush dissent and to silence whistleblowers.

The Ninth Amendment provides that people have other rights that may not be enumerated in the Bill of Rights, and the federal government is using the Ninth Amendment to create new rights, government-given rights, that defy the definition of rights which centers around Natural Law. As indicated in the Declaration of Independence, we are "endowed" by our "Creator" with "certain unalienable rights." That means that our rights are God-given, not government-given. Therefore, if our rights are God-given, then they must be God-defined, and that goes for the definition of what a Civil Right is, as well.

Rather than refraining itself from intruding upon our rights, or imposing itself upon local issues, through the guise of Civil Rights, the federal government has become a threat to freedom. The government is no longer acting with the "consent of the governed", nor is it abiding by the limiting principles established on the pages of the United States Constitution. The federal government is engaging in the authoritarian activities the Founding Fathers fought against, and much of it is in the name of protecting the "federal government defined" Civil Rights of a few select groups.

Recognizing the assault on personal liberties the expansion of the federal government has created, conservative groups and organizations have vowed to "resist the growth of federal power." Included in the fight to restore the republic, and resist the tyranny being perpetuated in the name of Civil Rights, is the proposal of a constitutional amendment enabling the States to overturn federal law with a two-thirds vote by the States. The "Repeal Amendment" was originally promoted by Virginia House Speaker Bill Howell in September of 2010, and passed the Virginia House of Delegates in January of 2011. In late 2015, the Repeal Amendment re-emerged, enumerated on a list of suggested amendments by Texas Governor Greg Abbott. The list accompanied Governor Abbott's call for an Article V. Convention.

Proponents of the "Repeal Amendment" claim that it provides a check on the ever-expanding federal government, protects against congressional overreach, and will get the government working for the people again. In turn, it could be used to also rebut the Civil Rights definitions being handed down by the federal government, enabling the States to reestablish their rightful role in the American System as sovereign, autonomous, unique, and individual entities.

People who call themselves "progressives" claim that the "Repeal Amendment" is contrary to what the United States Constitution represents. If conservatives are so adamant about how perfect the Constitution is as written, why would they seek to change it in such a drastic way?

In reality, the amendment supports authorities that the States already possess. The United States Congress already has the authority to defund, and impeach a president that is acting unconstitutionally; and using the Exceptions Clause in Article III, Congress may use legislation to make null and void any federal court ruling that they believe is contrary to the constitutional authorities granted to the federal government.

The States, also, possess authorities to stop a federal government using its self-proclaimed federal supremacy to force its own definition of Civil Rights upon the States. Nullification, and an Article V. Convention, along with grassroots efforts through local actions, can be used to disarm, and reverse, unconstitutional activities and definitions presented by the federal government.

The fears of the statists that inhabit the liberal left political ideology is that something like the Repeal Amendment, or recognizing State Sovereignty, will allow the States to misbehave again, like they did throughout the time period surrounding the War Between the States. The statist's claim is that if the States are given the kind of freedom they had originally under the United States Constitution, they would betray the Civil Rights of a great number of protected groups, and it would set this country back more than a century.

While the liberal left statists see the desire to embrace original intent as an unsafe fetish that would ultimately undo all of our advances to protect Civil Rights, those that support the Constitution see Civil Rights as a cultural issue that localism must work out for itself, without the forceful intrusions of an authoritarian federal government that claims its definitions of what a Civil Right is are the only acceptable definitions, regardless of what the governed say, or the churches preach.

CHAPTER 21

STATISM

Pronounced *stay-tism*, statism possesses many names, and many faces. During the time period surrounding the framing of the United States Constitution, statism was called utopianism, communitarianism, and nationalism. The redistribution of wealth was called "schemes of leveling." The early colonies, seeking a communal answer to combat the human trait of selfishness discovered early on that systems using a communal central storage quickly became poisoned by human nature, and hindered by those who refused to "pay their fair share."

Through researching history, the framers of the Constitution also came to the conclusion that a pure democracy, like communal systems, became a one way ticket to oligarchy – a statist system where a few political elites rule over the citizenry at large. Under such a system, citizenship and sovereignty are compromised, and the populace becomes mere subjects to the ruling regime.

When the Framers of the United States Constitution debated over the document that would create the federal government in Philadelphia during the summer of 1787, among the considerations that greatly influenced their decisions was human nature. The natural tendencies of human beings inspired the Framers of the Constitution to follow Montesquieu's advice about a Separation of Powers, Polybius's call for a mixed constitution, and the Saxon concepts of a division of powers and of Natural Rights. Human nature guides the way we react, the things we desire, and the realization of the insecurities we possess within us. Self-reliance and liberty take a lot of work, so we naturally lean towards utopia (statism), seeking a leader to do the things we feel are out of our hands. But, those same characteristics of human nature can negatively influence political leaders, moving them in a direction towards seeking power and wealth while propping themselves up as the all-knowing ruling elite that must protect freedom by taking it away.

Humans crave security, and we know that when left to our own devices without some kind of system to secure the rule of law, our rights are in constant danger. So, we create government knowing that without government there is no freedom. The Founding Fathers understood this reality, but also knew that limitations must be placed on government, for the application of too much government historically always limits freedom.

Government cannot create. Government cannot keep promises. Government cannot be innovative if centralized and allowed to become powerful. Government is operated by man, which means that all of the frailties of man, all of his shortcomings, and all of the other negative aspects of human nature are a part of government.

Government also does not possess the things that makes us special as individuals. Government cannot produce as a result of God-given talents or interests. Government does not have a drive to better itself, or to be personally responsible. Government does not have the self-interest to improve itself, or the desire to profit from its efforts so as to improve its line of business. The interests of government, in reality, are at odds with the interests of individualism.

Since government cannot produce, to function it must confiscate. When government "takes" from society, and reduces what is left of the fruits of individual production, it hinders the production of individuals. Under the threat of taking more, the producers produce less to guard against losing more. The end result is a government that betrays the means of production, and ultimately driving whole civilizations into poverty as the leviathan of government takes more and more until eventually, there is nothing left to take; and only misery remains to be given.

Government seeks to take more and more, and the production of individual ingenuity and innovative aspirations is reduced as a result. And as the wealth of liberty vanishes, the government is left with no other choice than to create perpetual debt in order to continue to operate. The debt increases as government expands, until there is no more value in the system to take. Then, still seeking more and more power, government begins to print fiat currency to fund its operations (and to manipulate the economy). As more money is printed and borrowed, the need to artificially hold up the economy increases. It becomes a vicious cycle that continuously devours itself in order to survive. Eventually, as the old saying goes, what goes up must come down.

The reality of collapse is recognized by the power-brokers in government, but the system has become too big. The progression of the expansion of government is addictive, and impossible to let go of. Everyone becomes the enemy, even the members of the citizenry. The government becomes paranoid, and they begin to institute security programs to protect their interests, and their ability to continue to expand. Eventually, criminal activity among the leadership is considered a necessary step to protecting their power. The ends justify the means. The rule of law becomes nothing more than an obstacle, and national security becomes a tool that can be manipulated and milked in order to gain more and more power. The sickness expands until the population is completely dependent upon government, and the desire to be an individual producer is killed. Ultimately, bondage is achieved, returning a society to its beginning, when tyranny ruled over it, and a few idealistic revolutionaries were willing to put on the line their lives, fortunes and sacred honor. . . not only for themselves, but especially for their posterity. . . for those not yet born.

The cycle is always the same. History is our guide. Tyranny always fails, and kills on its way to its own suicide. Such is the nature of statism.

CHAPTER 22

VIRTUOUS SOCIETY

Benjamin Franklin wisely determined that "Only a virtuous people are capable of freedom. As nations become corrupt and vicious, they have more need of masters."

Franklin may not be historically known as being a champion of theological thought, but his writings suggest that he not only recognized the importance of a civilization being grounded in some kind of system of moral values, but that as he got older he recognized the importance of praying to the Creator, and living one's life in line with the virtues provided by a Judeo-Christian foundation.

During the first few weeks of debate during the Federal Convention in 1787, the viciousness of the confrontations became so bad that the members of the delegation were getting no work accomplished towards the creation of a new United States Constitution. Benjamin Franklin, the elder statesman in the room, said nothing as the men battled. After about four weeks of quiet observation, Franklin finally spoke, providing godly encouragement the convention needed to become the "Miracle of Philadelphia" that would launch the greatest republic in history.

Benjamin Franklin is often referred to as a deist, or an agnostic. Franklin's faith is mysterious because there is ample evidence, mostly accented by his less-than-Christian actions (especially when it came to the ladies), that Franklin was not necessarily a devout Christian. Despite the questions surrounding the depth of Franklin's faith in God, his respect for Christianity and his recognition of the existence of the Judeo-Christian God is unmistakable.

One such example of his reverence towards the Christian religion emerged after Franklin's death. He was an ambassador to France from 1776 to 1785 and was a beloved figure among the French. In 1790, Jacques Mallet Du Pan, a French journalist and leader, indicated in his historical memoirs that Franklin had given the French political advice in regards to being a virtuous society. "Whoever should introduce the principles of primitive Christianity into the political state would change the whole order of society." An interesting piece of advice from the Pennsylvania statesman who is often considered a deist by historians.

As he got older, Dr. Franklin recognized the miracles that were emerging around him. These miracles left him no choice but to come to the conclusion that only divine Providence could be credited with the founding of the United States of America.

During the Constitutional Convention in 1787, after watching the failed debates of his combative colleagues, Franklin made an unexpected request. After four weeks of quiet observation, Franklin reminded his colleagues that they were on their knees during the American Revolution. He suggested that during the Constitution Convention, they should once again drop to their knees in prayer, and do so before each session of the convention.

"In this situation of this Assembly, groping as it were in the dark to find political truth, and scarce able to distinguish it when presented to us, how has it happened, Sir, that we have not hitherto once thought of humbly applying to the Father of lights to illuminate our understandings? In the beginning of the Contest with G. Britain, when we were sensible of danger we had daily prayer in this room for the divine protection.

Our prayers, Sir, were heard, and they were graciously answered. All of us who were engaged in the struggle must have observed frequent instances of a Superintending providence in our favor. To that kind providence we owe this happy opportunity of consulting in peace on the means of establishing our future national felicity. And have we now forgotten that powerful friend? I have lived, Sir, a long time, and the longer I live, the more convincing proofs I see of this truth - that God governs in the affairs of men. And if a sparrow cannot fall to the ground without his notice, is it probable that an empire can rise without his aid? We have been assured, Sir, in the sacred writings, that 'except the Lord build the House they labour in vain that build it.' I firmly believe this; and I also believe that without his concurring aid we shall succeed in this political building no better than the Builders of Babel: We shall be divided by our little partial local interests; our projects will be confounded, and we ourselves shall become a reproach and bye word down to future ages. And what is worse, mankind may hereafter from this unfortunate instance, despair of establishing Governments be Human Wisdom and leave it to chance, war and conquest."

Franklin's recommendation was debated for a few days, with Alexander Hamilton leading the opposition. After a couple days, however, it was decided that, though they could not afford a member of the clergy to lead them in prayer inside Independence Hall, they would walk down the street to the nearest church and appeal to heaven to give them the wisdom and the strength to construct a new constitution capable of standing the test of time, and protecting, preserving, and promoting the Union of sovereign States.

The tradition of prayer before each session of the United States Congress is directly tied to Franklin's request during the summer of 1787 in the Constitutional Convention.

The delegates generally recognized the truth in the same manner that Franklin did. Without a people being virtuous, freedom cannot be maintained. Without virtue, a culture will inevitably become something other than a virtuous society. Without the standards of morality being practiced in society, individuals seek corruption and violence. Therefore, as a result of the flawed nature of human nature, the new central government was limited in its scope and powers. The new American System was devised based on the structure of the Mosaic system presented in Deuteronomy of the Holy Bible, allowing the new federal government to only act upon certain authorities through the direct, or indirect, advice and consent of the States, the people, and the representatives of the people voted into office by direct, and indirect, election.

The trouble with creating a new central government is that historically, oligarchies always rise tyrannically through the centralization of government. Therefore, creating the new federal government involved a delicate balancing act. While a stronger government was needed in order to handle the external issues that the States were not able to accomplish individually, the new federal government also must be limited in such a manner that it did not eventually become a tyranny.

Virtue is an important part of that balancing act. Without a populace that is virtuous, moral, and informed, leaders seeking power may easily fool the people, encouraging them to vote into power those who would compromise their liberty.

As government seeks to expand, and virtue diminishes, society itself becomes a vicious place. To contain the corruption and violence, the expanding government increases the powers of law enforcement. The excuse is normally to preserve "the common good." Regimes seeking statism say they must force the violent and corrupt into submission, while in reality the increase of control is simply an authoritarian move towards a police state. With greater control being exhibited by the powerful ruling elite, eventually the society is doomed to become a system where the people are enslaved by powerful government forces, and tyrannical government regulations.

As the Tytler Cycle suggests, bondage cannot cease to be a condition of society unless there is a spiritual awakening, and it takes a spiritual awakening in order for a populace to become courageous enough to seek and achieve liberty, and the abundance that normally accompanies free systems. Without being a virtuous society, not only is bondage inevitable, but escaping bondage becomes impossible.

At the end of the Declaration of Independence, two phrases attract one's attention when considering the influence of God upon the endeavors of the Founding Fathers. They wrote, "And for the support of this Declaration, with a firm reliance on the protection of divine Providence, we mutually pledge to each other our Lives, Fortunes and sacred Honor."

As Franklin suggested, during the American Revolution, the founders recognized the importance of recognizing, and relying upon, the protection of God. Blanketed in protection, these men were willing to put on the line everything that was important to them, not only for themselves, but for their "Posterity" (those not yet born).

The final two words of the final sentence of the Declaration of Independence reveals how big the Founders realized their endeavor was. In addition to putting on the line their lives and fortunes, they were even willing to pledge to each other their "sacred Honor."

Sacred Honor is something much larger than mere honor. When we hear the word "honor," we think of persons that are honorable in the way they keep their word, and follow through with good and sound actions. Honor is something to be protected, as we see in the Japanese culture, and something to teach, as we have experienced in our own society. But, do we truly understand the next step up? At what point does honor become something that is sacred?

John Liberty of *Red State*, in his article titled, "Sacred Honor - The Last Words of the Declaration of Independence," wrote near the end of his article, "There is no honor in taking from others or in subjecting others to pain, suffering and tyranny. Honorable men have the ability to see tyranny and the backbone to stand against it, though all they own may be taken from them as they fight by whatever means necessary to ensure liberty for themselves and their fellow citizens. There is no more honorable pursuit than the cause of liberty for the common good."

Sacred Honor is a unique quality in the character of people, and of civilizations. Sacred Honor is not possible without a culture recognizing the difference between good and evil, without following some kind of Golden Rule (do onto others as you would have them do onto you), and sacred Honor is not possible in a society that is unwilling to act when confronted by evil.

The key in understanding sacred Honor is to also recognize that in order for a person, or a nation, to practice sacred Honor, they must be honorable in the first place.

According to the Founding Fathers, tyranny was something that not only needed to be resisted, but something they were willing to enter into a bloody revolution to resist.

Among today's deconstructionists, it is argued that according to their secular understanding of biblical dogmatism, it is sinful for Christians to rise up against a tyrannical government. They use this argument in order to try to prove that the Founding Fathers were not

Christians. Quoting Jesus, the deconstructionists tell us that we should "turn the other cheek," and that, as Romans 13 explains, "the powers that be are ordained of God."

In response, we recognize that God's higher powers supersedes man's highest powers, and for God to command unlimited submission to unjust government is a direct contradiction of God's nature.

Psalms 1:1-3 – "Blessed is the man that walketh not in the counsel of the ungodly, nor standeth in the way of sinners, nor sitteth in the seat of the scornful. But, his delight is in the law of the LORD, and in his law doth he meditate day and night. And he shall be like a tree planted by the rivers of water, that bringeth forth his fruit in not wither; and whatsoever he doeth shall prosper."

Psalms 2:1-3 – "Why do the heathen rage, and the people imagine a vain thing? The kings of the earth set themselves, and the rulers take counsel together, against the LORD, and against his anointed, saying, Let us break their bands asunder, and cast away their cords from us."

I Peter 5:8-9 – "Be sober, be vigilant; because your adversary the devil, as a roaring lion, walketh about: seeking whom he may devour: Whom resist stedfast in the faith, knowing that the same afflictions are accomplished in your brethren that are in the world"

It is clear that as a virtuous people we are commanded to resist evil. As our American System succumbs to tyrannical power-brokers, it is our duty (and our *right*, according to the Declaration of Independence), to "alter or abolish" the government, and "institute new Government, laying its foundation on such principles and organizing its powers in such form, as to them shall seem most likely to effect their Safety and Happiness." The Founding Fathers understood that to maintain a system of liberty, the citizenry must not only be moral and virtuous, but vigilant in protecting and preserving their liberty.

John Adams said, "Our Constitution was made only for a moral and religious people. It is wholly inadequate to the government of any other."

George Washington, in his Farewell Address, said, "Of all the dispositions and habits which lead to political prosperity, Religion and morality are indispensible supports."

Samuel Adams told us, "The sum of all is, if we would most truly enjoy the gift of Heaven, let us become a virtuous people; then shall we both deserve and enjoy it. While, on the other hand, if we are universally vicious and debauched in our manners, through the form of the Constitution carries the face of the most exalted freedom, we shall in reality be the most abject slaves."

In the Declaration of Independence, the term "sacred Honor" was not used lightly. The word "sacred" is a word that conveys the message that our Honor must be godly. The word "Honor" reminds us that we must do the honorable thing because it is the right thing to do.

If we are not a virtuous society, we are not capable of understanding concepts like natural rights, the rule of law, or the principles of limited government contained within the pages of our own United States Constitution. To adhere to a moral standard, we must recognize that the standard of morality exists in the first place, as does the concepts of good and evil, and right and wrong. If we are a people that follow such standards, our morality compels us to do what is right, to organize based on a rule of law that protects natural rights, and to follow the legal standards established by the Creator of the rule of law.

In the Declaration of Independence, Natural Law, and therefore our Natural Rights as members of a society that operates in accordance to the Rule of Law, are indicated as having four particular traits.

The first paragraph of the Declaration of Independence declares that the "Laws of Nature and of Nature's God entitle" the people to the "separate and equal station" of "the powers of the earth."

The second paragraph declares that these truths are "self-evident," we are "endowed by our Creator" with these truths, and that our rights are "unalienable."

In short, the following characteristics regarding our Natural Rights exist:

a) We are entitled to them;
b) Our rights are self-evident;
c) We are endowed by our Creator to have those Natural Rights (they are God-given);
d) And our Natural Rights are unalienable (we cannot be separated from them).

In order for our Natural Rights, and the Rule of Law, to be "self-evident," we must be able to recognize them in their original form. Only a virtuous society is capable of this. If they are self-evident, which means we are a virtuous society, then we will naturally recognize that we are entitled to our liberty, our rights are God-given, and that the principles of freedom and Natural Rights are unalienable.

The final question is simply, are we willing to defend liberty?

Final sentence of the Declaration of Independence:

"And for the support of this Declaration, with a firm reliance on the protection of divine Providence, we mutually pledge to each other our Lives, our Fortunes and our sacred Honor."

APPENDIX I

(Changed or obsolete passages in brackets)

The Constitution of the United States, 1787

Preamble

We the People of the United States, in Order to form a more perfect Union, establish Justice, insure domestic Tranquility, provide for the common defence, promote the general Welfare, and secure the Blessings of Liberty to ourselves and our Posterity, do ordain and establish this Constitution for the United States of America.

Article I

Section 1

All legislative Powers herein granted shall be vested in a Congress of the United States, which shall consist of a Senate and House of Representatives.

Section 2

The House of Representatives shall be composed of Members chosen every second Year by the People of the several States, and the Electors in each State shall have the Qualifications requisite for Electors of the most numerous Branch of the State

Legislature.

No Person shall be a Representative who shall not have attained to the Age of twenty five Years, and been seven Years a Citizen of the United States, and who shall not, when elected, be an Inhabitant of that State in which he shall be chosen.

[Representatives and direct Taxes shall be apportioned among the several States which may be included within this Union, according to their respective Numbers, which shall be determined by adding to the whole Number of free Persons, including those bound to Service for a Term of Years, and excluding Indians not taxed, three fifths of all other Persons.] *(Changed by section 2 of the Fourteenth Amendment)* The actual Enumeration shall be made within three Years after the first Meeting of the Congress of the United States, and within every subsequent Term of ten Years, in such Manner as they shall by Law direct. The Number of Representatives shall not exceed one for every thirty Thousand, but each State shall have at Least one Representative; and until such enumeration shall be made, the State of New Hampshire shall be entitled to chuse three, Massachusetts eight, Rhode-Island and Providence Plantations one, Connecticut five, New-York six, New Jersey four, Pennsylvania eight, Delaware one, Maryland six, Virginia ten, North Carolina five, South Carolina five, and Georgia three.

When vacancies happen in the Representation from

any State, the Executive Authority thereof shall issue Writs of Election to fill such Vacancies.

The House of Representatives shall chuse their Speaker and other Officers; and shall have the sole Power of Impeachment.

Section 3

The Senate of the United States shall be composed of two Senators from each State, [chosen by the Legislature thereof] *(Changed by the Seventeenth Amendment)* for six Years; and each Senator shall have one Vote.

Immediately after they shall be assembled in Consequence of the first Election, they shall be divided as equally as may be into three Classes. The Seats of the Senators of the first Class shall be vacated at the Expiration of the second Year, of the second Class at the Expiration of the fourth Year, and of the third Class at the Expiration of the sixth Year, so that one third may be chosen every second Year; [and if Vacancies happen by Resignation, or otherwise, during the Recess of the Legislature of any State, the Executive thereof may make temporary Appointments until the next Meeting of the Legislature, which shall then fill such Vacancies.] *(Changed by the Seventeenth Amendment)*

No Person shall be a Senator who shall not have attained to the Age of thirty Years, and been nine

Years a Citizen of the United States, and who shall not, when elected, be an Inhabitant of that State for which he shall be chosen.

The Vice President of the United States shall be President of the Senate, but shall have no Vote, unless they be equally divided.

The Senate shall chuse their other Officers, and also a President pro tempore, in the Absence of the Vice President, or when he shall exercise the Office of President of the United States.

The Senate shall have the sole Power to try all Impeachments. When sitting for that Purpose, they shall be on Oath or Affirmation. When the President of the United States is tried, the Chief Justice shall preside: And no Person shall be convicted without the Concurrence of two thirds of the Members present.

Judgment in Cases of Impeachment shall not extend further than to removal from Office, and disqualification to hold and enjoy any Office of honor, Trust or Profit under the United States: but the Party convicted shall nevertheless be liable and subject to Indictment, Trial, Judgment and Punishment, according to Law.

Section 4

The Times, Places and Manner of holding Elections for Senators and Representatives, shall be prescribed in each State by the Legislature thereof; but the Congress may at any time by Law make or alter such Regulations, except as to the Places of chusing Senators.

The Congress shall assemble at least once in every Year, and such Meeting shall be [on the first Monday in December,] *(Changed by Section 2 of the Twentieth Amendment)* unless they shall by Law appoint a different Day.

Section 5

Each House shall be the Judge of the Elections, Returns and Qualifications of its own Members, and a Majority of each shall constitute a Quorum to do Business; but a smaller Number may adjourn from day to day, and may be authorized to compel the Attendance of absent Members, in such Manner, and under such Penalties as each House may provide.

Each House may determine the Rules of its Proceedings, punish its Members for disorderly Behaviour, and, with the Concurrence of two thirds, expel a Member.

Each House shall keep a Journal of its Proceedings, and from time to time publish the same, excepting such Parts as may in their Judgment require Secrecy; and the Yeas and Nays of the Members of either House on any question shall, at the Desire of one fifth of those Present, be entered on the Journal.

Neither House, during the Session of Congress, shall, without the Consent of the other, adjourn for more than three days, nor to any other Place than that in which the two Houses shall be sitting.

Section 6

The Senators and Representatives shall receive a Compensation for their Services, to be ascertained by Law, and paid out of the Treasury of the United States. They shall in all Cases, except Treason, Felony and Breach of the Peace, be privileged from Arrest during their Attendance at the Session of their respective Houses, and in going to and returning from the same; and for any Speech or Debate in either House, they shall not be questioned in any other Place.

No Senator or Representative shall, during the Time for which he was elected, be appointed to any civil Office under the Authority of the United States, which shall have been created, or the Emoluments whereof shall have been encreased during such time; and no Person holding any Office under the United States, shall be a Member of either House during his Continuance in Office.

Section 7

All Bills for raising Revenue shall originate in the House of Representatives; but the Senate may propose or concur with Amendments as on other

Bills.

Every Bill which shall have passed the House of Representatives and the Senate, shall, before it become a Law, be presented to the President of the United States: If he approve he shall sign it, but if not he shall return it, with his Objections to that House in which it shall have originated, who shall enter the Objections at large on their Journal, and proceed to reconsider it. If after such Reconsideration two thirds of that House shall agree to pass the Bill, it shall be sent, together with the Objections, to the other House, by which it shall likewise be reconsidered, and if approved by two thirds of that House, it shall become a Law. But in all such Cases the Votes of both Houses shall be determined by yeas and Nays, and the Names of the Persons voting for and against the Bill shall be entered on the Journal of each House respectively. If any Bill shall not be returned by the President within ten Days (Sundays excepted) after it shall have been presented to him, the Same shall be a Law, in like Manner as if he had signed it, unless the Congress by their Adjournment prevent its Return, in which Case it shall not be a Law.

Every Order, Resolution, or Vote to which the Concurrence of the Senate and House of Representatives may be necessary (except on a question of Adjournment) shall be presented to the President of the United States; and before the Same shall take Effect, shall be approved by him, or being disapproved by him, shall be repassed by two thirds of the Senate and House of Representatives, according to the Rules and Limitations prescribed in the Case of a Bill.

Section 8

The Congress shall have Power To lay and collect Taxes, Duties, Imposts and Excises, to pay the Debts and provide for the common Defence and general Welfare of the United States; but all Duties, Imposts and Excises shall be uniform throughout the United States;

To borrow Money on the credit of the United States;

To regulate Commerce with foreign Nations, and among the several States, and with the Indian Tribes;

To establish an uniform Rule of Naturalization, and uniform Laws on the subject of Bankruptcies throughout the United States;

To coin Money, regulate the Value thereof, and of foreign Coin, and fix the Standard of Weights and Measures;

To provide for the Punishment of counterfeiting the Securities and current Coin of the United States;

To establish Post Offices and post Roads;

To promote the Progress of Science and useful Arts, by securing for limited Times to Authors and Inventors the exclusive Right to their respective Writings and Discoveries;

To constitute Tribunals inferior to the supreme Court;

To define and punish Piracies and Felonies committed on the high Seas, and Offences against the Law of Nations;

To declare War, grant Letters of Marque and Reprisal, and make Rules concerning Captures on Land and Water;

To raise and support Armies, but no Appropriation of Money to that Use shall be for a longer Term than two Years;

To provide and maintain a Navy;

To make Rules for the Government and Regulation of the land and naval Forces;

To provide for calling forth the Militia to execute the Laws of the Union, suppress Insurrections and repel Invasions;

To provide for organizing, arming, and disciplining, the Militia, and for governing such Part of them as may be employed in the Service of the United States, reserving to the States respectively, the

Appointment of the Officers, and the Authority of training the Militia according to the discipline prescribed by Congress;

To exercise exclusive Legislation in all Cases whatsoever, over such District (not exceeding ten Miles square) as may, by Cession of particular States, and the Acceptance of Congress, become the Seat of the Government of the United States, and to exercise like Authority over all Places purchased by the Consent of the Legislature of the State in which the Same shall be, for the Erection of Forts, Magazines, Arsenals, dock-Yards, and other needful Buildings;--And

To make all Laws which shall be necessary and proper for carrying into Execution the foregoing Powers, and all other Powers vested by this Constitution in the Government of the United States, or in any Department or Officer thereof.

Section 9

The Migration or Importation of such Persons as any of the States now existing shall think proper to admit, shall not be prohibited by the Congress prior to the Year one thousand eight hundred and eight, but a Tax or duty may be imposed on such Importation, not exceeding ten dollars for each Person.

The Privilege of the Writ of Habeas Corpus shall not be suspended, unless when in Cases of

Rebellion or Invasion the public Safety may require it.

No Bill of Attainder or ex post facto Law shall be passed.

No Capitation, or other direct, Tax shall be laid, unless in Proportion to the Census or enumeration herein before directed to be taken.

No Tax or Duty shall be laid on Articles exported from any State.

No Preference shall be given by any Regulation of Commerce or Revenue to the Ports of one State over those of another; nor shall Vessels bound to, or from, one State, be obliged to enter, clear, or pay Duties in another.

No Money shall be drawn from the Treasury, but in Consequence of Appropriations made by Law; and a regular Statement and Account of the Receipts and Expenditures of all public Money shall be published from time to time.

No Title of Nobility shall be granted by the United States: And no Person holding any Office of Profit or Trust under them, shall, without the Consent of the Congress, accept of any present, Emolument, Office, or Title, of any kind whatever, from any King, Prince, or foreign State.

Section 10

No State shall enter into any Treaty, Alliance, or Confederation; grant Letters of Marque and Reprisal; coin Money; emit Bills of Credit; make any Thing but gold and silver Coin a Tender in Payment of Debts; pass any Bill of Attainder, ex post facto Law, or Law impairing the Obligation of Contracts, or grant any Title of Nobility.

No State shall, without the Consent of the Congress, lay any Imposts or Duties on Imports or Exports, except what may be absolutely necessary for executing it's inspection Laws: and the net Produce of all Duties and Imposts, laid by any State on Imports or Exports, shall be for the Use of the Treasury of the United States; and all such Laws shall be subject to the Revision and Controul of the Congress.

No State shall, without the Consent of Congress, lay any Duty of Tonnage, keep Troops, or Ships of War in time of Peace, enter into any Agreement or Compact with another State, or with a foreign Power, or engage in War, unless actually invaded, or in such imminent Danger as will not admit of delay.

Article II

Section 1

The executive Power shall be vested in a President of the United States of America. He shall hold his Office during the Term of four Years, and, together with the Vice President, chosen for the same Term, be elected, as follows:

Each State shall appoint, in such Manner as the Legislature thereof may direct, a Number of Electors, equal to the whole Number of Senators and Representatives to which the State may be entitled in the Congress: but no Senator or Representative, or Person holding an Office of Trust or Profit under the United States, shall be appointed an Elector.

[The Electors shall meet in their respective States, and vote by Ballot for two Persons, of whom one at least shall not be an Inhabitant of the same State with themselves. And they shall make a List of all the Persons voted for, and of the Number of Votes for each; which List they shall sign and certify, and transmit sealed to the Seat of the Government of the United States, directed to the President of the Senate. The President of the Senate shall, in the Presence of the Senate and House of Representatives, open all the Certificates, and the Votes shall then be counted. The Person having the greatest Number of Votes shall be the President, if such Number be a Majority of the whole Number of Electors appointed; and if there be more than one who have such Majority, and have an equal Number of Votes, then the House of Representatives shall immediately chuse by Ballot one of them for President; and if no Person have a Majority, then from the five highest on the List the said House shall in like Manner chuse the President. But in chusing the President, the Votes shall be taken by States, the Representation from each State having one Vote; A quorum for this purpose shall consist of a Member or Members from two thirds of the States, and a Majority of all the States shall be necessary to a Choice. In every Case, after the Choice of the President, the Person having the greatest Number of Votes of the Electors shall be the Vice President. But if there should remain two or more who have equal Votes, the Senate shall chuse from them by Ballot the Vice President.] *(Changed by the Twelfth Amendment)*

The Congress may determine the Time of chusing the Electors, and the Day on which they shall give their Votes; which Day shall be the same throughout the United States.

No Person except a natural born Citizen, or a Citizen of the United States, at the time of the Adoption of this Constitution, shall be eligible to the Office of President; neither shall any Person be eligible to that Office who shall not have attained to the Age of thirty five Years, and been fourteen Years a Resident within the United States.

[In Case of the Removal of the President from Office, or of his Death, Resignation, or Inability to discharge the Powers and Duties of the said Office, the Same shall devolve on the Vice President, and the Congress may by Law provide for the Case of Removal, Death, Resignation or Inability, both of the President and Vice President, declaring what

Officer shall then act as President, and such Officer shall act accordingly, until the Disability be removed, or a President shall be elected.] *(Changed by the Twenty-Fifth Amendment)*

The President shall, at stated Times, receive for his Services, a Compensation, which shall neither be increased nor diminished during the Period for which he shall have been elected, and he shall not receive within that Period any other Emolument from the United States, or any of them.

Before he enter on the Execution of his Office, he shall take the following Oath or Affirmation:--"I do solemnly swear (or affirm) that I will faithfully execute the Office of President of the United States, and will to the best of my Ability, preserve, protect and defend the Constitution of the United States."

Section 2

The President shall be Commander in Chief of the Army and Navy of the United States, and of the Militia of the several States, when called into the actual Service of the United States; he may require the Opinion, in writing, of the principal Officer in each of the executive Departments, upon any Subject relating to the Duties of their respective Offices, and he shall have Power to grant Reprieves and Pardons for Offences against the United States, except in Cases of Impeachment.

He shall have Power, by and with the Advice and

Consent of the Senate, to make Treaties, provided two thirds of the Senators present concur; and he shall nominate, and by and with the Advice and Consent of the Senate, shall appoint Ambassadors, other public Ministers and Consuls, Judges of the supreme Court, and all other Officers of the United States, whose Appointments are not herein otherwise provided for, and which shall be established by Law: but the Congress may by Law vest the Appointment of such inferior Officers, as they think proper, in the President alone, in the Courts of Law, or in the Heads of Departments.

The President shall have Power to fill up all Vacancies that may happen during the Recess of the Senate, by granting Commissions which shall expire at the End of their next Session.

Section 3

He shall from time to time give to the Congress Information of the State of the Union, and recommend to their Consideration such Measures as he shall judge necessary and expedient; he may, on extraordinary Occasions, convene both Houses, or either of them, and in Case of Disagreement between them, with Respect to the Time of Adjournment, he may adjourn them to such Time as he shall think proper; he shall receive Ambassadors and other public Ministers; he shall take Care that the Laws be faithfully executed, and shall Commission all the Officers of the United States.

Section 4

The President, Vice President and all civil Officers of the United States, shall be removed from Office on Impeachment for, and Conviction of, Treason, Bribery, or other high Crimes and Misdemeanors.

Article III

Section 1

The judicial Power of the United States shall be vested in one supreme Court, and in such inferior Courts as the Congress may from time to time ordain and establish. The Judges, both of the supreme and inferior Courts, shall hold their Offices during good Behaviour, and shall, at stated Times, receive for their Services a Compensation, which shall not be diminished during their Continuance in Office.

Section 2

The judicial Power shall extend to all Cases, in Law and Equity, arising under this Constitution, the Laws of the United States, and Treaties made, or which shall be made, under their Authority;--to all Cases affecting Ambassadors, other public Ministers and Consuls;--to all Cases of admiralty and maritime Jurisdiction;--to Controversies to which the United States shall be a Party;--to Controversies between two or more States;-- [between a State and Citizens of another State,]

(Changed by the Eleventh Amendment) --between Citizens of different States,--between Citizens of the same State claiming Lands under Grants of different States, [and between a State, or the Citizens thereof, and foreign States, Citizens or Subjects.] *(Changed by the Eleventh Amendment)*

In all Cases affecting Ambassadors, other public Ministers and Consuls, and those in which a State shall be Party, the supreme Court shall have original Jurisdiction. In all the other Cases before mentioned, the supreme Court shall have appellate Jurisdiction, both as to Law and Fact, with such Exceptions, and under such Regulations as the Congress shall make.

The Trial of all Crimes, except in Cases of Impeachment, shall be by Jury; and such Trial shall be held in the State where the said Crimes shall have been committed; but when not committed within any State, the Trial shall be at such Place or Places as the Congress may by Law have directed.

Section 3

Treason against the United States, shall consist only in levying War against them, or in adhering to their Enemies, giving them Aid and Comfort. No Person shall be convicted of Treason unless on the Testimony of two Witnesses to the same overt Act, or on Confession in open Court.

The Congress shall have Power to declare the

Punishment of Treason, but no Attainder of Treason shall work Corruption of Blood, or Forfeiture except during the Life of the Person attainted.

Article IV

Section 1

Full Faith and Credit shall be given in each State to the public Acts, Records, and judicial Proceedings of every other State. And the Congress may by general Laws prescribe the Manner in which such Acts, Records and Proceedings shall be proved, and the Effect thereof.

Section 2

The Citizens of each State shall be entitled to all Privileges and Immunities of Citizens in the several States.

A Person charged in any State with Treason, Felony, or other Crime, who shall flee from Justice, and be found in another State, shall on Demand of the executive Authority of the State from which he fled, be delivered up, to be removed to the State having Jurisdiction of the Crime.

[No Person held to Service or Labour in one State, under the Laws thereof, escaping into another, shall, in Consequence of any Law or Regulation therein, be discharged from such Service or Labour, but shall be delivered up on Claim of the Party to whom such Service or Labour may be due.] *(Changed by the Thirteenth Amendment)*

Section 3

New States may be admitted by the Congress into this Union; but no new State shall be formed or erected within the Jurisdiction of any other State; nor any State be formed by the Junction of two or more States, or Parts of States, without the Consent of the Legislatures of the States concerned as well as of the Congress.

The Congress shall have Power to dispose of and make all needful Rules and Regulations respecting the Territory or other Property belonging to the United States; and nothing in this Constitution shall be so construed as to Prejudice any Claims of the United States, or of any particular State.

Section 4

The United States shall guarantee to every State in this Union a Republican Form of Government, and shall protect each of them against Invasion; and on Application of the Legislature, or of the Executive (when the Legislature cannot be convened), against domestic Violence.

Article V

The Congress, whenever two thirds of both Houses shall deem it necessary, shall propose Amendments to this Constitution, or, on the Application of the Legislatures of two thirds of the several States, shall call a Convention for proposing Amendments, which, in either Case, shall be valid to all Intents and Purposes, as Part of this Constitution, when ratified by the Legislatures of three fourths of the several States, or by Conventions in three fourths thereof, as the one or the other Mode of Ratification may be proposed by the Congress; Provided that no Amendment which may be made prior to the Year One thousand eight hundred and eight shall in any Manner affect the first and fourth Clauses in the Ninth Section of the first Article; and that no State, without its Consent, shall be deprived of its equal Suffrage in the Senate.

Article VI

All Debts contracted and Engagements entered into, before the Adoption of this Constitution, shall be as valid against the United States under this Constitution, as under the Confederation.

This Constitution, and the Laws of the United States which shall be made in Pursuance thereof; and all Treaties made, or which shall be made, under the Authority of the United States, shall be the supreme Law of the Land; and the Judges in every State shall be bound thereby, any Thing in the Constitution or Laws of any State to the Contrary notwithstanding.

The Senators and Representatives before mentioned, and the Members of the several State

Legislatures, and all executive and judicial Officers, both of the United States and of the several States, shall be bound by Oath or Affirmation, to support this Constitution; but no religious Test shall ever be required as a Qualification to any Office or public Trust under the United States.

Article VII

The Ratification of the Conventions of nine States, shall be sufficient for the Establishment of this Constitution between the States so ratifying the Same.

done in Convention by the Unanimous Consent of the States present the Seventeenth Day of September in the Year of our Lord one thousand seven hundred and Eighty seven and of the Independance of the United States of America the Twelfth In witness whereof We have hereunto subscribed our Names,

G°. Washington
Presidt and deputy from Virginia
New Hampshire
John Langdon
Nicholas Gilman

Massachusetts
Nathaniel Gorham
Rufus King

Connecticut

Wm. Saml. Johnson
Roger Sherman

New York
Alexander Hamilton

New Jersey
Wil: Livingston
David Brearley
Wm. Paterson
Jona: Dayton

Pennsylvania
B Franklin
Thomas Mifflin
Robt. Morris
Geo. Clymer
Thos. FitzSimons
Jared Ingersoll
James Wilson
Gouv Morris

Delaware
Geo: Read
Gunning Bedford jun
John Dickinson
Richard Bassett
Jaco: Broom

Maryland
James McHenry
Dan of St Thos. Jenifer
Danl. Carroll

Virginia
John Blair
James Madison Jr.

North Carolina
Wm. Blount
Richd. Dobbs Spaight
Hu Williamson

South Carolina
J. Rutledge
Charles Cotesworth Pinckney
Charles Pinckney
Pierce Butler

Georgia
William Few
Abr Baldwin

Attest William Jackson Secretary

Bill of Rights – Amendments 1-10, Ratified December 15, 1791

Amendment I

Congress shall make no law respecting an establishment of religion, or prohibiting the free exercise thereof; or abridging the freedom of speech, or of the press; or the right of the people peaceably to assemble, and to petition the Government for a redress of grievances.

Amendment II

A well regulated Militia, being necessary to the security of a free State, the right of the people to keep and bear Arms, shall not be infringed.

Amendment III

No Soldier shall, in time of peace be quartered in any house, without the consent of the Owner, nor in time of war, but in a manner to be prescribed by law.

Amendment IV

The right of the people to be secure in their persons, houses, papers, and effects, against unreasonable searches and seizures, shall not be violated, and no Warrants shall issue, but upon probable cause, supported by Oath or affirmation, and particularly describing the place to be searched, and the persons or things to be seized.

Amendment V

No person shall be held to answer for a capital, or otherwise infamous crime, unless on a presentment or indictment of a Grand Jury, except in cases arising in the land or naval forces, or in the Militia, when in actual service in time of War or public danger; nor shall any person be subject for the same offence to be twice put in jeopardy of life or limb; nor shall be compelled in any criminal case to be a witness against himself, nor be deprived of life, liberty, or property, without due process of law; nor shall private property be taken for public use, without just compensation.

Amendment VI

In all criminal prosecutions, the accused shall enjoy the right to a speedy and public trial, by an impartial jury of the State and district wherein the crime shall have been committed, which district shall have been previously ascertained by law, and to be informed of the nature and cause of the accusation; to be confronted with the witnesses against him; to have compulsory process for obtaining witnesses in his favor, and to have the Assistance of Counsel for his defence.

Amendment VII

In Suits at common law, where the value in

controversy shall exceed twenty dollars, the right of trial by jury shall be preserved, and no fact tried by a jury, shall be otherwise re-examined in any Court of the United States, than according to the rules of the common law.

Amendment VIII

Excessive bail shall not be required, nor excessive fines imposed, nor cruel and unusual punishments inflicted.

Amendment IX

The enumeration in the Constitution, of certain rights, shall not be construed to deny or disparage others retained by the people.

Amendment X

The powers not delegated to the United States by the Constitution, nor prohibited by it to the States, are reserved to the States respectively, or to the people.

Amendments 11-27

Amendment XI

Passed by Congress March 4, 1794. Ratified February 7, 1795.

The Judicial power of the United States shall not be

construed to extend to any suit in law or equity, commenced or prosecuted against one of the United States by Citizens of another State, or by Citizens or Subjects of any Foreign State.

Amendment XII

Passed by Congress December 9, 1803. Ratified June 15, 1804.

The Electors shall meet in their respective states and vote by ballot for President and Vice-President, one of whom, at least, shall not be an inhabitant of the same state with themselves; they shall name in their ballots the person voted for as President, and in distinct ballots the person voted for as Vice-President, and they shall make distinct lists of all persons voted for as President, and of all persons voted for as Vice-President, and of the number of votes for each, which lists they shall sign and certify, and transmit sealed to the seat of the government of the United States, directed to the President of the Senate; -- the President of the Senate shall, in the presence of the Senate and House of Representatives, open all the certificates and the votes shall then be counted; -- The person having the greatest number of votes for President, shall be the President, if such number be a majority of the whole number of Electors appointed; and if no person have such majority, then from the persons having the highest numbers not exceeding three on the list of those voted for as President, the House of Representatives shall choose immediately, by ballot, the President. But in choosing the President, the votes shall be taken by states, the representation from each state having one vote; a quorum for this purpose shall consist of a member or members from two-thirds of the states, and a majority of all the states shall be necessary to a choice. [And if the House of Representatives shall not choose a President whenever the right of choice shall devolve upon them, before the fourth day of March next following, then the Vice-President shall act as President, as in case of the death or other constitutional disability of the President. –] *(Superseded by section 3 of the Twentieth Amendment)* The person having the greatest number of votes as Vice-President, shall be the Vice-President, if such number be a majority of the whole number of Electors appointed, and if no person have a majority, then from the two highest numbers on the list, the Senate shall choose the Vice-President; a quorum for the purpose shall consist of two-thirds of the whole number of Senators, and a majority of the whole number shall be necessary to a choice. But no person constitutionally ineligible to the office of President shall be eligible to that of Vice-President of the United States.

Amendment XIII

Passed by Congress January 31, 1865. Ratified December 6, 1865.

Section 1.
Neither slavery nor involuntary servitude, except as

a punishment for crime whereof the party shall have been duly convicted, shall exist within the United States, or any place subject to their jurisdiction.

Section 2.
Congress shall have power to enforce this article by appropriate legislation.

Amendment XIV

Passed by Congress June 13, 1866. Ratified July 9, 1868.

Section 1.
All persons born or naturalized in the United States, and subject to the jurisdiction thereof, are citizens of the United States and of the State wherein they reside. No State shall make or enforce any law which shall abridge the privileges or immunities of citizens of the United States; nor shall any State deprive any person of life, liberty, or property, without due process of law; nor deny to any person within its jurisdiction the equal protection of the laws.

Section 2.
Representatives shall be apportioned among the several States according to their respective numbers, counting the whole number of persons in each State, excluding Indians not taxed. But when the right to vote at any election for the choice of electors for President and Vice-President of the United States, Representatives in Congress, the

Executive and Judicial officers of a State, or the members of the Legislature thereof, is denied to any of the male inhabitants of such State, [being twenty-one years of age,] *(Changed by section 1 of the 26th amendment)* and citizens of the United States, or in any way abridged, except for participation in rebellion, or other crime, the basis of representation therein shall be reduced in the proportion which the number of such male citizens shall bear to the whole number of male citizens twenty-one years of age in such State.

Section 3.
No person shall be a Senator or Representative in Congress, or elector of President and Vice-President, or hold any office, civil or military, under the United States, or under any State, who, having previously taken an oath, as a member of Congress, or as an officer of the United States, or as a member of any State legislature, or as an executive or judicial officer of any State, to support the Constitution of the United States, shall have engaged in insurrection or rebellion against the same, or given aid or comfort to the enemies thereof. But Congress may by a vote of two-thirds of each House, remove such disability.

Section 4.
The validity of the public debt of the United States, authorized by law, including debts incurred for payment of pensions and bounties for services in suppressing insurrection or rebellion, shall not be questioned. But neither the United States nor any

State shall assume or pay any debt or obligation incurred in aid of insurrection or rebellion against the United States, or any claim for the loss or emancipation of any slave; but all such debts, obligations and claims shall be held illegal and void.

Section 5.
The Congress shall have the power to enforce, by appropriate legislation, the provisions of this article.

Amendment XV

Passed by Congress February 26, 1869. Ratified February 3, 1870.

Section 1.
The right of citizens of the United States to vote shall not be denied or abridged by the United States or by any State on account of race, color, or previous condition of servitude--

Section 2.
The Congress shall have the power to enforce this article by appropriate legislation.

Amendment XVI

Passed by Congress July 2, 1909. Ratified February 3, 1913.

The Congress shall have power to lay and collect taxes on incomes, from whatever source derived, without apportionment among the several States, and without regard to any census or enumeration.

Amendment XVII

Passed by Congress May 13, 1912. Ratified April 8, 1913.

The Senate of the United States shall be composed of two Senators from each State, elected by the people thereof, for six years; and each Senator shall have one vote. The electors in each State shall have the qualifications requisite for electors of the most numerous branch of the State legislatures.

When vacancies happen in the representation of any State in the Senate, the executive authority of such State shall issue writs of election to fill such vacancies: Provided, That the legislature of any State may empower the executive thereof to make temporary appointments until the people fill the vacancies by election as the legislature may direct.

This amendment shall not be so construed as to affect the election or term of any Senator chosen before it becomes valid as part of the Constitution.

Amendment XVIII

Passed by Congress December 18, 1917. Ratified January 16, 1919.

[Section 1.

After one year from the ratification of this article the manufacture, sale, or transportation of intoxicating liquors within, the importation thereof into, or the exportation thereof from the United States and all territory subject to the jurisdiction thereof for beverage purposes is hereby prohibited.

Section 2.
The Congress and the several States shall have concurrent power to enforce this article by appropriate legislation.

Section 3.
This article shall be inoperative unless it shall have been ratified as an amendment to the Constitution by the legislatures of the several States, as provided in the Constitution, within seven years from the date of the submission hereof to the States by the Congress.] *(Repealed by amendment 21)*

Amendment XIX

Passed by Congress June 4, 1919. Ratified August 18, 1920.

The right of citizens of the United States to vote shall not be denied or abridged by the United States or by any State on account of sex.

Congress shall have power to enforce this article by appropriate legislation.

Amendment XX

Passed by Congress March 2, 1932. Ratified January 23, 1933.

Section 1.
The terms of the President and the Vice President shall end at noon on the 20th day of January, and the terms of Senators and Representatives at noon on the 3rd day of January, of the years in which such terms would have ended if this article had not been ratified; and the terms of their successors shall then begin.

Section 2.
The Congress shall assemble at least once in every year, and such meeting shall begin at noon on the 3d day of January, unless they shall by law appoint a different day.

Section 3.
If, at the time fixed for the beginning of the term of the President, the President elect shall have died, the Vice President elect shall become President. If a President shall not have been chosen before the time fixed for the beginning of his term, or if the President elect shall have failed to qualify, then the Vice President elect shall act as President until a President shall have qualified; and the Congress may by law provide for the case wherein neither a President elect nor a Vice President shall have qualified, declaring who shall then act as President, or the manner in which one who is to act shall be selected, and such person shall act accordingly until

a President or Vice President shall have qualified.

Section 4.
The Congress may by law provide for the case of the death of any of the persons from whom the House of Representatives may choose a President whenever the right of choice shall have devolved upon them, and for the case of the death of any of the persons from whom the Senate may choose a Vice President whenever the right of choice shall have devolved upon them.

Section 5.
Sections 1 and 2 shall take effect on the 15th day of October following the ratification of this article.

Section 6.
This article shall be inoperative unless it shall have been ratified as an amendment to the Constitution by the legislatures of three-fourths of the several States within seven years from the date of its submission.

Amendment XXI

Passed by Congress February 20, 1933. Ratified December 5, 1933.

Section 1.
The eighteenth article of amendment to the Constitution of the United States is hereby repealed.

Section 2.

The transportation or importation into any State, Territory, or Possession of the United States for delivery or use therein of intoxicating liquors, in violation of the laws thereof, is hereby prohibited.

Section 3.
This article shall be inoperative unless it shall have been ratified as an amendment to the Constitution by conventions in the several States, as provided in the Constitution, within seven years from the date of the submission hereof to the States by the Congress.

Amendment XXII

Passed by Congress March 21, 1947. Ratified February 27, 1951.

Section 1.
No person shall be elected to the office of the President more than twice, and no person who has held the office of President, or acted as President, for more than two years of a term to which some other person was elected President shall be elected to the office of President more than once. But this Article shall not apply to any person holding the office of President when this Article was proposed by Congress, and shall not prevent any person who may be holding the office of President, or acting as President, during the term within which this Article becomes operative from holding the office of President or acting as President during the remainder of such term.

Section 2.
This article shall be inoperative unless it shall have been ratified as an amendment to the Constitution by the legislatures of three-fourths of the several States within seven years from the date of its submission to the States by the Congress.

Amendment XXIII

Passed by Congress June 16, 1960. Ratified March 29, 1961.

Section 1.
The District constituting the seat of Government of the United States shall appoint in such manner as Congress may direct:

A number of electors of President and Vice President equal to the whole number of Senators and Representatives in Congress to which the District would be entitled if it were a State, but in no event more than the least populous State; they shall be in addition to those appointed by the States, but they shall be considered, for the purposes of the election of President and Vice President, to be electors appointed by a State; and they shall meet in the District and perform such duties as provided by the twelfth article of amendment.

Section 2.
The Congress shall have power to enforce this article by appropriate legislation.

Amendment XXIV

Passed by Congress August 27, 1962. Ratified January 23, 1964.

Section 1.
The right of citizens of the United States to vote in any primary or other election for President or Vice President, for electors for President or Vice President, or for Senator or Representative in Congress, shall not be denied or abridged by the United States or any State by reason of failure to pay poll tax or other tax.

Section 2.
The Congress shall have power to enforce this article by appropriate legislation.

Amendment XXV

Passed by Congress July 6, 1965. Ratified February 10, 1967.

Section 1.
In case of the removal of the President from office or of his death or resignation, the Vice President shall become President.

Section 2.
Whenever there is a vacancy in the office of the Vice President, the President shall nominate a Vice President who shall take office upon confirmation

by a majority vote of both Houses of Congress.

Section 3.
Whenever the President transmits to the President pro tempore of the Senate and the Speaker of the House of Representatives his written declaration that he is unable to discharge the powers and duties of his office, and until he transmits to them a written declaration to the contrary, such powers and duties shall be discharged by the Vice President as Acting President.

Section 4.
Whenever the Vice President and a majority of either the principal officers of the executive departments or of such other body as Congress may by law provide, transmit to the President pro tempore of the Senate and the Speaker of the House of Representatives their written declaration that the President is unable to discharge the powers and duties of his office, the Vice President shall immediately assume the powers and duties of the office as Acting President.

Thereafter, when the President transmits to the President pro tempore of the Senate and the Speaker of the House of Representatives his written declaration that no inability exists, he shall resume the powers and duties of his office unless the Vice President and a majority of either the principal officers of the executive department or of such other body as Congress may by law provide, transmit within four days to the President pro tempore of the

Senate and the Speaker of the House of Representatives their written declaration that the President is unable to discharge the powers and duties of his office. Thereupon Congress shall decide the issue, assembling within forty-eight hours for that purpose if not in session. If the Congress, within twenty-one days after receipt of the latter written declaration, or, if Congress is not in session, within twenty-one days after Congress is required to assemble, determines by two-thirds vote of both Houses that the President is unable to discharge the powers and duties of his office, the Vice President shall continue to discharge the same as Acting President; otherwise, the President shall resume the powers and duties of his office.

Amendment XXVI

Passed by Congress March 23, 1971. Ratified July 1, 1971.

Section 1.
The right of citizens of the United States, who are eighteen years of age or older, to vote shall not be denied or abridged by the United States or by any State on account of age.

Section 2.
The Congress shall have power to enforce this article by appropriate legislation.

Amendment XXVII

Originally proposed Sept. 25, 1789. Ratified May 7, 1992.

No law, varying the compensation for the services of the Senators and Representatives, shall take effect, until an election of representatives shall have intervened.

Note: Congress submitted the text of the Twenty-Seventh Amendment to the States as part of the proposed Bill of Rights on September 25, 1789. The Amendment was not ratified together with the first Ten Amendments, which became effective on December 15, 1791. The Twenty-Seventh Amendment was ratified on May 7, 1992, by the vote of Michigan.

APPENDIX II

The Declaration of Independence

IN CONGRESS, July 4, 1776.

The unanimous Declaration of the thirteen united States of America,

When in the Course of human events, it becomes necessary for one people to dissolve the political bands which have connected them with another, and to assume among the powers of the earth, the separate and equal station to which the Laws of Nature and of Nature's God entitle them, a decent respect to the opinions of mankind requires that they should declare the causes which impel them to the separation.

We hold these truths to be self-evident, that all men are created equal, that they are endowed by their Creator with certain unalienable Rights, that among these are Life, Liberty and the pursuit of Happiness.--That to secure these rights, Governments are instituted among Men, deriving their just powers from the consent of the governed, --That whenever any Form of Government becomes destructive of these ends, it is the Right of the People to alter or to abolish it, and to institute new Government, laying its foundation on such principles and organizing its powers in such form, as to them shall seem most likely to effect their Safety and Happiness. Prudence, indeed, will dictate that Governments long established should not be changed for light and transient causes; and accordingly all experience hath shewn, that mankind are more disposed to suffer, while evils are sufferable, than to right themselves by abolishing the forms to which they are accustomed. But when a long train of abuses and usurpations, pursuing invariably the same Object evinces a design to reduce them under absolute Despotism, it is their right, it is their duty, to throw off such Government, and to provide new Guards for their future security.--Such has been the patient sufferance of these Colonies; and such is now the necessity which constrains them to alter their former Systems of Government. The history of the present King of Great Britain is a history of repeated injuries and usurpations, all having in direct object the establishment of an absolute Tyranny over these States. To prove this, let Facts be submitted to a candid world.

He has refused his Assent to Laws, the most wholesome and necessary for the public good.

He has forbidden his Governors to pass Laws of immediate and pressing importance, unless suspended in their operation till his Assent should be obtained; and when so suspended, he has utterly neglected to attend to them.

He has refused to pass other Laws for the accommodation of large districts of people, unless those people would relinquish the right of Representation in the Legislature, a right inestimable to them and formidable to tyrants only.

He has called together legislative bodies at

places unusual, uncomfortable, and distant from the depository of their public Records, for the sole purpose of fatiguing them into compliance with his measures.

He has dissolved Representative Houses repeatedly, for opposing with manly firmness his invasions on the rights of the people.

He has refused for a long time, after such dissolutions, to cause others to be elected; whereby the Legislative powers, incapable of Annihilation, have returned to the People at large for their exercise; the State remaining in the mean time exposed to all the dangers of invasion from without, and convulsions within.

He has endeavoured to prevent the population of these States; for that purpose obstructing the Laws for Naturalization of Foreigners; refusing to pass others to encourage their migrations hither, and raising the conditions of new Appropriations of Lands.

He has obstructed the Administration of Justice, by refusing his Assent to Laws for establishing Judiciary powers.

He has made Judges dependent on his Will alone, for the tenure of their offices, and the amount and payment of their salaries.

He has erected a multitude of New Offices, and sent hither swarms of Officers to harrass our people, and eat out their substance.

He has kept among us, in times of peace, Standing Armies without the Consent of our legislatures.

He has affected to render the Military

independent of and superior to the Civil power.

He has combined with others to subject us to a jurisdiction foreign to our constitution, and unacknowledged by our laws; giving his Assent to their Acts of pretended Legislation:

For Quartering large bodies of armed troops among us:

For protecting them, by a mock Trial, from punishment for any Murders which they should commit on the Inhabitants of these States:

For cutting off our Trade with all parts of the world:

For imposing Taxes on us without our Consent:

For depriving us in many cases, of the benefits of Trial by Jury:

For transporting us beyond Seas to be tried for pretended offences

For abolishing the free System of English Laws in a neighbouring Province, establishing therein an Arbitrary government, and enlarging its Boundaries so as to render it at once an example and fit instrument for introducing the same absolute rule into these Colonies:

For taking away our Charters, abolishing our most valuable Laws, and altering fundamentally the Forms of our Governments:

For suspending our own Legislatures, and declaring themselves invested with power to legislate for us in all cases whatsoever.

He has abdicated Government here, by declaring us out of his Protection and waging War against us.

He has plundered our seas, ravaged our Coasts,

burnt our towns, and destroyed the lives of our people.

He is at this time transporting large Armies of foreign Mercenaries to compleat the works of death, desolation and tyranny, already begun with circumstances of Cruelty & perfidy scarcely paralleled in the most barbarous ages, and totally unworthy the Head of a civilized nation.

He has constrained our fellow Citizens taken Captive on the high Seas to bear Arms against their Country, to become the executioners of their friends and Brethren, or to fall themselves by their Hands.

He has excited domestic insurrections amongst us, and has endeavoured to bring on the inhabitants of our frontiers, the merciless Indian Savages, whose known rule of warfare, is an undistinguished destruction of all ages, sexes and conditions.

In every stage of these Oppressions We have Petitioned for Redress in the most humble terms: Our repeated Petitions have been answered only by repeated injury. A Prince whose character is thus marked by every act which may define a Tyrant, is unfit to be the ruler of a free people.

Nor have We been wanting in attentions to our Brittish brethren. We have warned them from time to time of attempts by their legislature to extend an unwarrantable jurisdiction over us. We have reminded them of the circumstances of our emigration and settlement here. We have appealed to their native justice and magnanimity, and we have conjured them by the ties of our common kindred to disavow these usurpations, which, would inevitably interrupt our connections and correspondence. They too have been deaf to the voice of justice and of consanguinity. We must, therefore, acquiesce in the necessity, which denounces our Separation, and hold them, as we hold the rest of mankind, Enemies in War, in Peace Friends.

We, therefore, the Representatives of the united States of America, in General Congress, Assembled, appealing to the Supreme Judge of the world for the rectitude of our intentions, do, in the Name, and by Authority of the good People of these Colonies, solemnly publish and declare, That these United Colonies are, and of Right ought to be Free and Independent States; that they are Absolved from all Allegiance to the British Crown, and that all political connection between them and the State of Great Britain, is and ought to be totally dissolved; and that as Free and Independent States, they have full Power to levy War, conclude Peace, contract Alliances, establish Commerce, and to do all other Acts and Things which Independent States may of right do. And for the support of this Declaration, with a firm reliance on the protection of divine Providence, we mutually pledge to each other our Lives, our Fortunes and our sacred Honor.

The 56 signatures on the Declaration appear in the positions indicated:

Column 1
Georgia:
  Button Gwinnett
  Lyman Hall
  George Walton

Column 2
North Carolina:
  William Hooper
  Joseph Hewes
  John Penn
South Carolina:
  Edward Rutledge
  Thomas Heyward, Jr.
  Thomas Lynch, Jr.
  Arthur Middleton

Column 3
Massachusetts:
John Hancock
Maryland:
Samuel Chase
William Paca
Thomas Stone
Charles Carroll of Carrollton
Virginia:
George Wythe
Richard Henry Lee
Thomas Jefferson
Benjamin Harrison
Thomas Nelson, Jr.
Francis Lightfoot Lee
Carter Braxton

Column 4
Pennsylvania:
Robert Morris
Benjamin Rush
Benjamin Franklin
John Morton
George Clymer
James Smith
George Taylor
James Wilson
George Ross
Delaware:
Caesar Rodney
George Read
Thomas McKean

Column 5
New York:
William Floyd
Philip Livingston
Francis Lewis
Lewis Morris
New Jersey:
Richard Stockton
John Witherspoon
Francis Hopkinson
John Hart
Abraham Clark

Column 6
New Hampshire:

Josiah Bartlett
William Whipple
Massachusetts:
Samuel Adams
John Adams
Robert Treat Paine
Elbridge Gerry

Rhode Island:
Stephen Hopkins
William Ellery
Connecticut:
Roger Sherman
Samuel Huntington
William Williams
Oliver Wolcott
New Hampshire:
Matthew Thornton

ABOUT THE AUTHOR

Douglas V. Gibbs is an author, columnist, radio host, instructor, television contributor, blogger and public speaker.   www.douglasvgibbs.com

OTHER BOOKS BY DOUGLAS V. GIBBS

25 Myths of the United States Constitution

The Basic Constitution: An Examination of the Principles and Philosophies of the United States Constitution

Silenced Screams: Abortion in a Virtuous Society

Made in the USA
Columbia, SC
24 August 2022